SCENES FROM SHAKESPEARE

Fifteen Cuttings for the Classroom

by

MICHAEL WILSON

MERIWETHER PUBLISHING LTD.
Colorado Springs, Colorado

Meriwether Publishing Ltd., Publisher
P.O. Box 7710
Colorado Springs, CO 80933

Executive Editor: Theodore O. Zapel
Typesetting: Susan Trinko
Cover design: Tom Myers

Library of Congress Cataloging-in-Publication Data

Shakespeare, William, 1564-1616.
    [Plays. Selections]
    Scenes from Shakespeare : fifteen cuttings for the classroom / [compiled] by Michael Wilson. -- 1st ed.
        p.   cm.
    Summary: A collection of fifteen short scenes from five Shakespeare plays: "Romeo and Juliet," "The Merchant of Venice," "Julius Caesar," "Othello," and "Hamlet." Each scene is preceded by a plot synopsis and descriptions of the characters.
    ISBN 0-916260-90-9 : $9.95
    1.   Shakespeare,   William,   1564-1616--Outlines,   syllabi,   etc.
2. Shakespeare, William, 1564-1616--Quotations. 3. Quotations, English.
4. Drama in education.   [1. Shakespeare, William, 1564-1616--Outlines, syllabi, etc. 2. Plays.]   I. Wilson, Michael, 1952-   .   II. Title.
PR2987.S45   1993
822.3'3--dc20   93-223
                                                                  CIP
                                                                  AC

This book is lovingly dedicated to
my wife Celeste
my son Jared
and my daughter Vanessa

ACKNOWLEDGMENTS

I would like to extend a special "thank you" to the following people who, in one way or another, helped or influenced me in this project: my mother and father, Ray and Chris Barnes; George and Joyce Cowie; Jim Watts; Wayne Stone; Tim McFadden; Dick Doepker, principal of Golden West High School; Dr. Ted Postelle, head of the Golden West English Department; Paul Jones, Noble Johnson, and Steve LaMar from the College of the Sequoias Drama Department (for your constant support, advice, and inspiration); Rev. Harry Wood; Mark and Marla Alberstein; Steve Lourence; my Advanced Drama Production class for allowing me to use you as "guinea pigs" for this project and for being such wonderful people.

Above all, extra special thanks to Sam Anderson — it was your guiding hand that led me to the stage door for the very first time so many years ago.

Michael Wilson

TABLE OF CONTENTS

Introduction vii

Note to the Teacher viii

Romeo and Juliet — Act II, Scene 1 1

Romeo and Juliet — Act III, Scene 1 11

Romeo and Juliet — Act V, Scene 3 19

The Merchant of Venice — Act I, Scene 2 27

The Merchant of Venice — Act I, Scene 3 32

Julius Caesar — Act II, Scene 2 39

Julius Caesar — Act III, Scene 2 46

Othello — Act III, Scene 3 57

Othello — Act III, Scene 4 75

Hamlet — Act I, Scene 1 84

Hamlet — Act I, Scene 2 91

Hamlet — Act I, Scene 5 102

Hamlet — Act III, Scene 1 110

Hamlet — Act III, Scene 4 117

Hamlet — Act IV, Scene 7 127

About the Author 135

INTRODUCTION

I have been teaching Shakespeare for 12 years and, until now, could not find a way to teach the beauty of the language along with the texts of the actor in a three- to four-week unit. Normally, I would teach an entire play, such as *Hamlet, The Merchant of Venice,* or *Othello,* read the entire script, discuss it, break the play down into workable scenes, rehearse and memorize, and perform it as an in-class project. However, this process would usually take six weeks, and by the time the performance was scheduled, my students would be "burned out."

This book is designed for use by drama teachers at the high school and junior college level: it presents the material in a structure that will allow the student success without the "long, tedious struggle" (as some of my students have said it!).

Here's how it works: I have chosen several scenes from various plays, making sure that they were relatively small in cast size. Each scene contains between two and seven characters. At the beginning of each scene I have written the names of characters, a brief description of each character, the major and minor characters in the scene (let's face it — not everyone wants the lead!), and, most importantly, a description of what has occurred thus far in the play; in other words, if a student is cast as Iago in *Othello* and is assigned to perform Act II, Scene 4, he reads the description and he should know his setting, basic character development, and motivation. Then, after enough rehearsal time, the students can perform these in class (each scene is between 15 and 25 minutes in length).

I used these scenes in my Advanced Drama Production class and found that the students performed better, were more enthusiastic, and felt more success than they ever had before. It is my hope that your students will discover the wonders of Shakespeare throughout this book.

NOTE TO THE TEACHER

I did not include elements of the Subtext, such as tone, timing, pacing, actions, movement, and emphasis and progression; I feel that each teacher has his or her methods for doing so. However, some excellent books that I have used for reference are *How Tall is This Ghost, John?*, (copyright © 1984 by the Australian Assoc. for the Teaching of English, Hyde Park Press Pty Ltd., Adelaide), by David Mallick; and *Shakescenes*, (copyright © 1992 by Applause Theatre Book Publishers of New York), by John Russell Brown.

Romeo and Juliet
Act II, Scene 1

MAJOR CHARACTERS

Romeo — a romantic, sensitive, and passionate young man, probably 16 or 17 years old

Juliet — a romantic young girl, approximately 14 years old

MINOR CHARACTERS

Benvolio — a Montague and companion to Romeo

Mercutio — a Montague and companion to Romeo

EXTRA — **Nurse**

This scene, the balcony scene, is one of the most famous in all of Shakespeare's works. Though containing only two characters, its passion, spontaneity, and romantic declaration make it stand alone in audience appeal. According to Thomas Marc Parrot, professor of English at Princeton University, "No other play, no other passage, seems to have appealed so strongly to the college youth of the 17th century, and what was true then has remained true ever since. In all the fluctuating phases of taste and judgment in succeeding centuries, *Romeo and Juliet* has survived as the supreme expression of the supreme and characteristic passion of youth, the passion of instinctive, romantic, world-forgetting love. The play is the work of Shakespeare's youth, his first utterance in the field of romantic tragedy, and it has remained ever since the poem best loved by romantic youth."

The basic story line, up to this point, is as follows: the setting is Verona, Italy, in the 14th century. The town's two prominent families, the Capulets and the Montagues, are in the midst of a serious feud. Romeo, a Montague, has (earlier in the story) confessed his love-sick heart to his cousin Benvolio. His romantic involvement with another woman has recently been severed, and Benvolio, hoping to ease his pain by finding him another lover, invites him to a masquerade ball in order to "examine other beauties." The problem, however, is that the ball is being held at the home of the Capulets.

It is there that Romeo spots Juliet and, as the saying goes, falls instantly in love with her. He speaks with her, and it becomes apparent that she, too, is equal in attraction to him. They kiss, but do so discreetly because of the social situation and setting. However, they discover that they belong to the families of their "great enemy" — he is a Montague and she is a Capulet.

This scene takes place later that evening. After the ball, Romeo aimlessly wanders the streets cursing his fate. (He says, in Act I, Scene 5, "Is she a Capulet? O dear account! My life is my foe's debt!") He finds himself outside the walls of the Capulet orchard; boldly, he climbs the wall and leaps down within the Capulet property.

Then, he sees her: it is Juliet walking out onto her balcony. At first he hides to hear her speak. After he listens to his "bright angel" confess her love and devotion for him, he emerges from his hiding place and climbs up the balcony to her. It is there that they dedicate themselves to one another and pledge the faith of undying love.

It is essential that this scene is performed honestly, spontaneously, and with passion. Don't overplay it with melodramatic movements, nor should it be underplayed by not incorporating touching and playful passion. Remember, these are two teenagers that are engulfed in overwhelming emotions that, at the present time, they are too enamored with to control.

1 *AT RISE:* Enter Romeo alone.

2

3 ROMEO: **Can I go forward when my heart is here?**

4 **Turn back, dull earth, and find thy center out.** *(He retires.*

5 *Enter BENVOLIO with MERCUTIO)*

6 BENVOLIO: **Romeo, my cousin Romeo! Romeo!**

7 MERCUTIO: **He's wise and on my life hath stol'n him home**

8 **to bed.**

9 BENVOLIO: **He ran this way and leapt this orchard wall.**

10 **Call, good Mercutio.**

11 MERCUTIO: **Nay I'll conjure too.**

12 **Romeo! humors! madman! passion! lover!**

13 **Appear thou in the likeness of a sigh,**

14 **Speak but one rhyme and I am satisfy'd,**

15 **Cry but "Ay me!" pronounce but "love" and "dove,"**

16 **Speak to my goship Venus one fair word,**

17 **One nickname for her purblind son and heir.**

18 **Young Abram Cupid, he that shot so true**

19 **When King Cophetua lov'd the beggar maid.**

20 **He heareth not, he stirreth not, he moveth not:**

21 **The ape is dead and I must conjure him.**

22 **I conjure thee by Rosaline's bright eyes,**

23 **By her high forehead and her scarlet lip,**

24 **By her fine foot, straight leg and quiv'ring thigh,**

25 **And the demesnes that there adjacent lie,**

26 **That in thy likeness thou appear to us.**

27 BENVOLIO: **And if he hear thee thou wilt anger him.**

28 MERCUTIO: **This cannot anger him. 'Twould anger him**

29 **To raise a spirit in his mistress' circle**

30 **Of some strange nature, letting it there stand**

31 **Till she had laid it and conjur'd it down —**

32 **That were some spite. My invocation**

33 **Is fair and honest, in his mistress' name**

34 **I conjure only but to raise up him.**

35 BENVOLIO: **Come, he hath hid himself among these trees**

1 To be consorted with the hum'rous night.
2 Blind is his love and best befits the dark.
3 MERCUTIO: If love be blind love cannot hit the mark.
4 Now will he sit under a medlar tree
5 And wish his mistress were that kind of fruit
6 As maids call medlars when they laugh alone.
7 O Romeo, that she were — O that she were
8 An open-arse or thou a pop'rin pear.
9 Romeo, good night. I'll to my truckle-bed,
10 This field-bed is too cold for me to sleep.
11 Come, shall we go?
12 BENVOLIO: Go then, for 'tis in vain
13 To seek him here that means not to be found. *(Exit*
14 *BENVOLIO and MERCUTIO)*
15 ROMEO: He jests at scars that never felt a wound.
16 But soft, what light through yonder window breaks?
17 It is the East and Juliet is the sun.
18 Arise fair Sun and kill the envious Moon,
19 Who is already sick and pale with grief
20 That thou her maid art far more fair than she.
21 Be not her maid, since she is envious,
22 Her vestal liv'ry is but sick and green,
23 And none but fools do wear it, cast it off. *(Enter JULIET*
24 *at the window)*
25 It is my lady! O it is my love!
26 O that she knew she were!
27 She speaks yet she says nothing, what of that?
28 Her eye discourses, I will answer it.
29 I am too bold, 'tis not to me she speaks.
30 Two of the fairest stars in all the heaven,
31 Having some business, do entreat her eyes
32 To twinkle in their spheres till they return.
33 What if her eyes were there, they in her head?
34 The brightness of her cheek would shame those stars
35 As daylight doth a lamp; her eye in heaven

1	Would through the airy region stream so bright
2	That birds would sing and think it were not night.
3	See how she leans her cheek upon her hand!
4	O that I were a glove upon that hand
5	That I might touch that cheek.
6	JULIET: Ay me!
7	ROMEO: She speaks.
8	O speak again, bright angel, for thou art
9	As glorious to this night, being o'er my head,
10	As is a winged messenger of Heaven
11	Unto the white-upturned wond'ring eyes
12	Of mortals that fall back to gaze on him
13	When he bestrides the lazy puffing clouds
14	And sails upon the bosom of the air.
15	JULIET: O Romeo, Romeo, wherefore art thou Romeo?
16	Deny thy father and refuse thy name;
17	Or if thou wilt not, be but sworn my love
18	And I'll no longer be a Capulet.
19	ROMEO: Shall I hear more or shall I speak at this?
20	JULIET: 'Tis but thy name that is my enemy,
21	Thou art thyself, though not a Montague.
22	What's Montague? it is nor hand nor foot
23	Nor arm nor face, O be some other name
24	Belonging to a man.
25	What's in a name? that which we call a rose
26	By any other word would smell as sweet.
27	So Romeo would, were he not Romeo call'd,
28	Retain that dear perfection which he owes
29	Without that title. Romeo, doff thy name,
30	And for thy name, which is no part of thee,
31	Take all myself.
32	ROMEO: I take thee at thy word.
33	Call me but Love and I'll be new baptiz'd,
34	Henceforth I never will be Romeo.
35	JULIET: What man art thou that thus bescreen'd in night

1   So stumblest on my counsel?

2   ROMEO: By a name

3   I know not how to tell thee who I am.

4   My name, dear saint, is hateful to myself

5   Because it is an enemy to thee.

6   Had I it written, I would tear the word.

7   JULIET: My ears have yet not drunk a hundred words

8   Of thy tongue's utt'ring, yet I know the sound.

9   Art thou not Romeo, and a Montague?

10   ROMEO: Neither, fair maid, if either thee dislike.

11   JULIET: How cam'st thou hither, tell me, and wherefore?

12   The orchard walls are high and hard to climb,

13   And the place death, considering who thou art,

14   If any of my kinsmen find thee here.

15   ROMEO: With Love's light wings did I o'erperch these walls,

16   For stony limits cannot hold Love out,

17   And what Love can do, that dares Love attempt.

18   Therefore thy kinsmen are no stop to me.

19   JULIET: If they do see thee they will murther thee.

20   ROMEO: Alack, there lies more peril in thine eye

21   Than twenty of their swords, look thou but sweet

22   And I am proof against their enmity.

23   JULIET: I would not for the world they saw thee here.

24   ROMEO: I have night's cloak to hide me from their eyes,

25   And but thou love me, let them find me here.

26   My life were better ended by their hate

27   Than death prorogued, wanting of thy love.

28   JULIET: By whose direction found'st thou out this place?

29   ROMEO: By Love, that first did prompt me to inquire.

30   He lent me counsel, and I lent him eyes.

31   I am no pilot, yet wert thou as far

32   As that vast shore wash'd with the farthest sea,

33   I should adventure for such marchandise.

34   JULIET: Thou know'st the mask of night is on my face,

35   Else would a maiden blush bepaint my cheek

1	For that which thou hast heard me speak tonight.
2	Fain would I dwell on form — fain, fain deny
3	What I have spoke. But farewell compliment.
4	Dost thou love me? I know thou wilt say "Ay,"
5	And I will take thy word. Yet if thou swear'st
6	Thou mayst prove false — at lovers' perjuries
7	They say Jove laughs. O gentle Romeo,
8	If thou dost love pronounce it faithfully —
9	Or if thou think'st I am too quickly won,
10	I'll frown and be perverse and say thee nay,
11	So thou wilt woo; but else, not for the world.
12	In truth, fair Montague, I am too fond,
13	And therefore thou mayst think my havior light,
14	But trust me, gentleman, I'll prove more true
15	Than those that have more cunning to be strange.
16	I should have been more strange, I must confess,
17	But that thou overheard'st, ere I was ware,
18	My true-love passion. Therefore pardon me,
19	And not impute this yielding to light love,
20	Which the dark night hath so discovered.
21	ROMEO: Lady, by yonder blessed moon I vow,
22	That tips with silver all these fruit-tree tops —
23	JULIET: O swear not by the moon, th' inconstant moon,
24	That monthly changes in her circl'd orb,
25	Lest that thy love prove likewise variable.
26	ROMEO: What shall I swear by?
27	JULIET: Do not swear at all,
28	Or if thou wilt, swear by thy gracious self,
29	Which is the god of my idolatry,
30	And I'll believe thee.
31	ROMEO: If my heart's dear love —
32	JULIET: Well, do not swear. Although I joy in thee
33	I have no joy of this contract tonight.
34	It is too rash, too unadvis'd, too sudden,
35	Too like the lightning, which doth cease to be

1   Ere one can say "It lightens." Sweet, good night.
2   This bud of love by Summer's rip'ning breath
3   May prove a beauteous flow'r when next we meet.
4   Good night, good night! As sweet repose and rest
5   Come to thy heart as that within my breast.
6   ROMEO: O wilt thou leave me so unsatisfy'd?
7   JULIET: What satisfaction canst thou have tonight?
8   ROMEO: Th' exchange of thy love's faithful vow for mine.
9   JULIET: I gave thee mine before thou didst request it,
10   And yet I would it were to give again.
11   ROMEO: Wouldst thou withdraw it? For what purpose, love?
12   JULIET: But to be frank and give it thee again.
13   And yet I wish but for the thing I have,
14   My bounty is as boundless as the sea,
15   My love as deep — the more I give to thee
16   The more I have, for both are infinite.
17   I hear some noise within. Dear love, adieu — *(NURSE calls*
18   *within.)*
19   Anon, good Nurse! Sweet Montague, be true.
20   Stay but a little, I will come again. *(Exit JULIET)*
21   ROMEO: O blessed blessed night! I am afear'd,
22   Being in night, all this is but a dream
23   Too flatt'ring sweet to be substantial. *(Enter JULIET)*
24   JULIET: Three words, dear Romeo, and good night indeed.
25   If that thy bent of love be hon'rable,
26   Thy purpose marriage, send me word tomorrow
27   By one that I'll procure to come to thee
28   Where and what time thou wilt perform the rite,
29   And all my fortunes at thy foot I'll lay
30   And follow thee my lord throughout the world.
31   NURSE: *(Within)* Madam!
32   JULIET: I come, anon. But if thou mean'st not well,
33   I do beseech thee —
34   NURSE: *(Within)* Madam!
35   JULIET: By and by I come.

1   — To cease thy strife and leave me to my grief.
2   Tomorrow will I send.
3   ROMEO: So thrive my soul.
4   JULIET: A thousand times good night. *(Exit JULIET)*
5   ROMEO: A thousand times the worse to want thy light!
6   Love goes toward love as schoolboys from their books,
7   But love from love toward school with heavy looks. *(Enter*
8   *JULIET again.)*
9   JULIET: Hist Romeo, hist! O for a falkner's voice
10   To lure this tassel-gentle back again.
11   Bondage is hoarse and may not speak aloud,
12   Else would I tear the cave where Echo lies
13   And make her airy tongue more hoarse than mine
14   With repetition of my Romeo.
15   ROMEO: It is my soul that calls upon my name.
16   How silver-sweet sound lovers' tongues by night,
17   Like softest music to attending ears.
18   JULIET: Romeo —
19   ROMEO: My dear?
20   JULIET: What a clock tomorrow
21   Shall I send to thee?
22   ROMEO: By the hour of nine.
23   JULIET: I will not fail, 'tis twenty year till then.
24   I have forgot why I did call thee back.
25   ROMEO: Let me stand here till thou remember it.
26   JULIET: I shall forget, to have thee still stand there,
27   Rememb'ring how I love thy company.
28   ROMEO: And I'll still stay, to have thee still forget,
29   Forgetting any other home but this.
30   JULIET: 'Tis almost morning. I would have thee gone,
31   And yet no farther than a wanton's bird
32   That lets it hop a little from his hand,
33   Like a poor pris'ner in his twisted gyves,
34   And with a silken threed plucks't back again,
35   So loving-jealous of his liberty.

1   **ROMEO:**   I would I were thy bird.

2   **JULIET:**   Sweet, so would I,

3   Yet I should kill thee with much cherishing.

4   Good night, good night!

5   **ROMEO:**   Parting is such sweet sorrow

6   That I shall say good night till it be morrow.

7   **JULIET:**   Sleep dwell upon thine eyes, peace in thy breast —

8   Would I were sleep and peace, so sweet to rest! *(Exit JULIET)*

9   **ROMEO:**   The grey-ey'd Morn smiles on the frowning Night,

10   Check'ring the eastern clouds with streaks of light,

11   And fleckled Darkness like a drunkard reels

12   From forth Day's path and Titan's burning wheels.

13   Hence will I to my ghostly Friar's close cell,

14   His help to crave and my dear hap to tell. *(Exit ROMEO)*

15

16

17

18

19

20

21

22

23

24

25

26

27

28

29

30

31

32

33

34

35

Romeo and Juliet
Act III, Scene 1

MAJOR CHARACTERS

Mercutio — a Montague and companion to Romeo. He is friendly, humorous, and quite a talker.

Benvolio — a Montague and companion to Romeo. He is probably the most logical and level-headed character in the play.

Tybalt — a Capulet; he is hot-tempered and quick to fight.

MINOR CHARACTERS

Lady Capulet — Juliet's mother; aunt to Tybalt

Old Montague — Romeo's father

Prince Escalus — the ruler of Verona. He has already warned the two families to stop fighting in Act I, Scene 1: "If ever you disturb our streets again, your lives shall pay the forfeit of the peace."

EXTRAS — Petruchio, citizens

This scene is an exciting one to play because it involves stage fighting. Because of the scene's outcome, it is also considered to be the turning point of the play.

Here is what has transpired thus far: Romeo, a Montague, has met and fallen in love with Juliet, a Capulet, at a masquerade ball. The obvious problem arises here when one realizes that the Montagues and Capulets hate one another and have been feuding for years. Romeo leaves the ball and later speaks to her at her balcony; there he confesses his love and undying devotion to her and she does the same to him. Romeo makes arrangements with Friar Lawrence to marry Juliet, and they do so in private.

As this scene opens, the quarreling families are about to square off and fight. Romeo enters just as Tybalt and Mercutio draw their swords to one another. Romeo tries to stop the fight, not only because the Prince has strictly prohibited fighting in Verona's streets, but now he is related to Tybalt (by way of his secret marriage to Juliet) and wants no bloodshed on either family side.

However, as he tries to stop the brawl, Tybalt stabs Mercutio while Romeo is blocking the latter's view; in his fury, Romeo, in turn, kills Tybalt and flees.

After the deaths, Prince Escalus bans Romeo from Verona, thus preventing Romeo from ever seeing his new bride again. This will prove to be a punishment worse than death for Romeo. (After hearing of his banishment, Romeo says, "Ha, banishment! Be merciful, say death; for exile hath more terror in his look, much more than death!" Act III, Scene 3)

When staging this scene, work slowly when choreographing the fighting. Don't telegraph the moves too much, but rehearse it well enough to know what the fighters are doing. This should be fast-paced until the Prince enters, and his speech should be angry and firm, thus turning the dynamics of the scene.

1   *AT RISE:*   Enter Mercutio, Benvolio and Men.

2

3   BENVOLIO: I pray thee good Mercutio, let's retire. The day

4   is hot, the Capels are abroad, and if we meet we shall not

5   scape a brawl, for now these hot days is the mad blood

6   stirring.

7   MERCUTIO: Thou art like one of these fellows that, when he

8   enters the confines of a tavern, claps me his sword upon

9   the table and say, "God send me no need of thee" — and

10   by the operation of the second cup draws him on the

11   drawer, when indeed there is no need.

12   BENVOLIO: Am I like such a fellow?

13   MERCUTIO: Come, come, thou art as hot a Jack in thy mood

14   as any in Italy, and as soon moved to be moody and as

15   soon moody to be moved.

16   BENVOLIO: And what to?

17   MERCUTIO: Nay, and there were two such we should have

18   none shortly, for one would kill the other. Thou? — why

19   thou wilt quarrel with a man that hath a hair more or a

20   hair less in his beard than thou hast. Thou wilt quarrel

21   with a man for cracking nuts, having no other reason but

22   because thou hast hazel eyes. What eye but such an eye

23   would spy out such a quarrel? Thy head is as full of quarrels

24   as an egg is full of meat, and yet thy head hath been beaten

25   as addle as an egg for quarreling. Thou hast quarrel'd

26   with a man for coughing in the street, because he hath

27   waken'd thy dog that hath lain asleep in the sun. Didst

28   thou not fall out with a tailor for wearing his new doublet

29   before Easter? With another for tying his new shoes with

30   old riband? And yet thou wilt tutor me from quarreling!

31   BENVOLIO: And I were so apt to quarrel as thou art, any

32   man should buy the fee-simple of my life for an hour and

33   a quarter.

34   MERCUTIO: The fee-simple? O simple! *(Enter TYBALT,*

35   *PETRUCHIO and others)*

1   BENVOLIO: By my head, here comes the Capulets.

2   MERCUTIO: By my heel, I care not.

3   TYBALT: Follow me close, for I will speak to them.

4   Gentlemen, good den, a word with one of you.

5   MERCUTIO: And but one word with one of us? Couple it with

6   something. Make it a word and a blow.

7   TYBALT: You shall find me apt enough to that, sir, and you

8   will give me occasion.

9   MERCUTIO: Could you not take some occasion without

10   giving?

11   TYBALT: Mercutio, thou consort'st with Romeo.

12   MERCUTIO: Consort? What! Dost thou make us minstrels?

13   And thou make minstrels of us, look to hear nothing but

14   discords. Here's my fiddlestick, here's that shall make you

15   dance. Zounds, consort!

16   BENVOLIO: We talk here in the public haunt of men.

17   Either withdraw unto some private place

18   Or reason coldly of your grievances

19   Or else depart. Here all eyes gaze on us.

20   MERCUTIO: Men's eyes were made to look, and let them gaze,

21   I will not budge for no man's pleasure, I. *(Enter ROMEO)*

22   TYBALT: Well, peace be with you, sir, here comes my man.

23   MERCUTIO: But I'll be hang'd sir, if he wear your livery.

24   Marry, go before to field, he'll be your follower,

25   Your worship in that sense may call him "man."

26   TYBALT: Romeo, the love I bear thee can afford

27   No better term than this, thou art a villain

28   ROMEO: Tybalt, the reason that I have to love thee

29   Doth much excuse the appertaining rage

30   To such a greeting. Villain am I none,

31   Therefore farewell, I see thou know'st me not.

32   TYBALT: Boy, this shall not excuse the injuries

33   That thou hast done me, therefore turn and draw.

34   ROMEO: I do protest I never injur'd thee,

35   But love thee better than thou canst devise

1   Till thou shalt know the reason of my love.

2   And so, good Capulet (which name I tender

3   As dearly as mine own) be satisfy'd.

4 MERCUTIO: O calm, dishon'rable, vile submission!

5   *Alla stoccatho* carries it away!

6   Tybalt, you ratcatcher, will you walk?

7 TYBALT: What wouldst thou have with me?

8 MERCUTIO: Good King of Cats, nothing but one of your nine

9   lives, that I mean to make bold withal and (as you shall

10   use me hereafter) dry-beat the rest of the eight. Will you

11   pluck your sword out of his pilcher by the ears? Make

12   haste, lest mine be about your ears ere it be out.

13 TYBALT: I am for you.

14 ROMEO: Gentle Mercutio, put thy rapier up.

15 MERCUTIO: Come sir, your *passado!* *(They fight.)*

16 ROMEO: Draw, Benvolio, beat down their weapons.

17   Gentlemen, for shame forbear this outrage.

18   Tybalt, Mercutio! The Prince expressly hath

19   Forbid this bandying in Verona streets.

20   Hold, Tybalt! Good Mercutio! *(TYBALT, under ROMEO's*

21   *arm, thrusts MERCUTIO in and flies.)*

22 MERCUTIO: I am hurt.

23   A plague a both houses, I am sped.

24   Is he gone and hath nothing?

25 BENVOLIO: What! art thou hurt?

26 MERCUTIO: Ay, ay, a scratch, a scratch, marry, 'tis enough.

27   Where is my page? Go villain, fetch a surgeon. *(Exit PAGE)*

28 ROMEO: Courage man, the hurt cannot be much.

29 MERCUTIO: No, 'tis not so deep as a well nor so wide as a

30   church door, but 'tis enough, 'twill serve — ask for me

31   tomorrow and you shall find me a grave man. I am

32   peppered, I warrant, for this world. A plague a both your

33   houses! Zounds! A dog, a rat, a mouse, a cat, to scratch a

34   man to death! A braggart, a rogue, a villain that fights by

35   the book of arithmetic! Why the devil came you between

1	us? I was hurt under your arm.
2	ROMEO: I thought all for the best.
3	MERCUTIO: Help me into some house, Benvolio,
4	Or I shall faint. A plague a both your houses.
5	They have made worms' meat of me.
6	I have it, and soundly too. Your houses! *(Exit MERCUTIO*
7	*and BENVOLIO)*
8	ROMEO: This gentleman, the Prince's near ally,
9	My very friend, hath got this mortal hurt
10	In my behalf, my reputation stain'd
11	With Tybalt's slander — Tybalt, that an hour
12	Hath been my cousin. O sweet Juliet,
13	Thy beauty hath made me effeminate,
14	And in my temper soften'd valor's steel. *(Enter BENVOLIO)*
15	BENVOLIO: O Romeo, Romeo, brave Mercutio's dead.
16	That gallant spirit hath aspir'd the clouds,
17	Which too untimely here did scorn the earth.
18	ROMEO: This day's black fate on moe days doth depend,
19	This but begins the woe others must end. *(Enter TYBALT)*
20	BENVOLIO: Here comes the furious Tybalt back again.
21	ROMEO: He gay in triumph, and Mercutio slain!
22	Away to Heav'n, respective lenity,
23	And fire-ey'd Fury be my conduct now!
24	Now Tybalt, take the "villain" back again
25	That late thou gav'st me, for Mercutio's soul
26	Is but a little way above our heads,
27	Staying for thine to keep him company.
28	Either thou or I or both must go with him.
29	TYBALT: Thou wretched boy that didst consort him here
30	Shalt with him hence.
31	ROMEO: This shall determine that. *(They fight. TYBALT falls.)*
32	BENVOLIO: Romeo, away, be gone!
33	The Citizens are up and Tybalt slain.
34	Stand not amaz'd, the Prince will doom thee death
35	If thou art taken. Hence, be gone, away!

1 ROMEO: O I am Fortune's fool!
2 BENVOLIO: Why dost thou stay? *(Exit ROMEO. Enter*
3   *CITIZENS)*
4 CITIZENS: Which way ran he that kill'd Mercutio?
5   Tybalt, that murtherer, which way ran he?
6 BENVOLIO: There lies that Tybalt.
7 CITIZEN: Up sir, go with me.
8   I charge thee in the Prince's name obey. *(Enter PRINCE,*
9   *OLD MONTAGUE, CAPULET, their WIVES and all)*
10 PRINCE: Where are the vile beginners of this fray?
11 BENVOLIO: O noble Prince, I can discover all
12   Th' unlucky manage of this fatal brawl.
13   There lies the man, slain by young Romeo,
14   That slew thy kinsman, brave Mercutio.
15 CAPULET'S WIFE: Tybalt, my cousin! O my brother's child!
16   O Prince! O husband! O the blood is spill'd
17   Of my dear kinsman! Prince, as thou art true,
18   For blood of ours shed blood of Montague.
19   O cousin, cousin!
20 PRINCE: Benvolio, who began this bloody fray?
21 BENVOLIO: Tybalt here slain, whom Romeo's hand did slay.
22   Romeo that spoke him fair bid him bethink
23   How nice the quarrrel was and urg'd withal
24   Your high displeasure. All this uttered
25   With gentle breath, calm look, knees humbly bow'd,
26   Could not take truce with the unruly spleen
27   Of Tybalt, deaf to peace, but that he tilts
28   With piercing steel at bold Mercutio's breast,
29   Who all as hot turns deadly point to point
30   And with a martial scorn with one hand beats
31   Cold death aside and with the other sends
32   It back to Tybalt, whose dexterity
33   Retorts it. Romeo he cries aloud,
34   "Hold, friends! Friends, part!" And swifter than his tongue
35   His agile arm beats down their fatal points

1	And 'twixt them rushes; underneath whose arm
2	An envious thrust from Tybalt hit the life
3	Of stout Mercutio; and then Tybalt fled,
4	But by and by comes back to Romeo,
5	Who had but newly entertain'd revenge,
6	And to 't they go like lightning; for ere I
7	Could draw to part them was stout Tybalt slain,
8	And as he fell did Romeo turn and fly.
9	This is the truth or let Benvolio die.
10	CAPULET'S WIFE: He is a kinsman to the Montague,
11	Affection makes him false, he speaks not true.
12	Some twenty of them fought in this black strife,
13	And all those twenty could but kill one life.
14	I beg for justice, which thou, Prince, must give —
15	Romeo slew Tybalt, Romeo must not live.
16	PRINCE: Romeo slew him, he slew Mercutio.
17	Who now the price of his dear blood doth owe?
18	MONTAGUE: Not Romeo, Prince, he was Mercutio's friend.
19	His fault concludes but what the law should end —
20	The life of Tybalt.
21	PRINCE: And for that offence
22	Immediately we do exile him hence.
23	I have an int'rest in your hate's proceeding,
24	My blood for your rude brawls doth lie a-bleeding.
25	But I'll amerce you with so strong a fine
26	That you shall all repent the loss of mine.
27	I will be deaf to pleading and excuses,
28	Nor tears nor prayers shall purchase out abuses.
29	Therefore use none. Let Romeo hence in haste,
30	Else when he's found that hour is his last.
31	Bear hence this body and attend our will.
32	Mercy but murders, pardoning those that kill. *(All exit.)*
33	
34	
35	

Romeo and Juliet
Act V, Scene 3

MAJOR CHARACTERS

Paris — the gentleman who was to marry Juliet (arranged by Juliet's father); he is civil, upright, and honorable.

Romeo — the 17-year-old lover of Juliet; at this part of the play he is guided only by his desperate attempt to reunite with Juliet, his new bride.

Juliet — the 14-year-old bride of Romeo. She is lying in the Capulet tomb in a death-like state that was induced by drinking a potion given to her by Friar Lawrence. She is desperately in love with Romeo.

MINOR CHARACTERS

Balthasar — Romeo's serving boy and messenger

Friar Lawrence — the kind-hearted and well-intentioned Friar who not only married Romeo and Juliet, but devised the plan for them to reunite.

EXTRAS — Paris' page, first watchman

This is the final climactic scene in the play. Here is what has thus transpired: the story takes place in the 14th century in Verona, Italy, amid a feud between two prominent families — the Montagues and the Capulets. Romeo, a Montague, has fallen in love with Juliet, a Capulet. He speaks to Friar Lawrence, a local monk, and convinces him to marry them in secret.

The day after the secret ceremony takes place, Romeo comes upon a fight about to begin between Mercutio, his cousin, and Tybalt, Juliet's quick-tempered and fiery cousin. Romeo tries to stop the battle, not only because the Prince has strictly prohibited fighting in Verona's streets, but now he is related to Tybalt (by way of his secret marriage to Juliet) and wants no bloodshed on either family side. He stops the fracas, and when Mercutio's vision of Tybalt is blocked by Romeo, Tybalt stabs Mercutio and kills him. In his fury, Romeo kills Tybalt and flees.

Prince Escalus arrives immediately after Romeo flees and, as punishment for killing Tybalt, banishes him from Verona, thus preventing him from being with his new bride, Juliet.

Friar Lawrence, the kind monk who married the two, devises a plan to reunite the lovers: he will give Juliet a potion that will put her into a deep sleep for 42 hours; when her nurse tries to awaken her, she will assume that Juliet has died. (The potion will cause "a cold and drowsy humor shall run through all thy veins; no warmth, no breath, shall testify thou livest.") Juliet's body shall then be placed in the Capulet family tomb, and Romeo (who is presently in the town of Mantua) shall be notified of the plan and will go to the tomb when she awakes and take her to Mantua where they will live happily forevermore.

However, two events occur that thwart the plan: first, the message never reaches Romeo. The messenger, Friar John, was suspected of having a highly contagious disease and was quarantined and confined to remain in residence. Second, Balthasar, a friend of Romeo, sees Juliet's body being placed in the tomb and logically assumes that she is dead.

When Romeo hears of her "death," he becomes distraught. (Remember, he has no idea of the Friar's plan.) He then goes to an apothecary (druggist), buys some poison, and goes to Juliet's tomb. Outside the Capulet's vaults, he sees Paris, the man who Lord Capulet had arranged to marry Juliet. Paris assumes that Romeo, who is a Montague and has been banished for killing Tybalt, is here to do "villainous shame to the dead bodies." He tries to apprehend Romeo, but in their struggle, Romeo kills him.

Romeo enters the vault and sees Juliet's body. He delivers his final soliloquy, takes the poison and dies. Shortly thereafter, Juliet awakens from her deep sleep. She sees Romeo's dead body, and, taking his dagger, kills herself.

This scene is indeed a challenge and will require mature actors. Be careful not to overplay this scene; portray it honestly and convincingly. Romeo's final soliloquy is beautiful and poignant, and Juliet's closing words are some of the most memorable in theatre.

1	***AT RISE:*** Enter Paris and his Page (with flowers and sweet water).
2	
3	**PARIS:** **Give me thy torch, boy, hence and stand aloof.**
4	**Yet put it out, for I would not be seen.**
5	**Under yond yew trees lay thee all along,**
6	**Holding thy ear close to the hollow ground,**
7	**So shall no foot upon the churchyard tread**
8	**(Being loose, unfirm with digging up of graves)**
9	**But thou shalt hear it. Whistle then to me**
10	**As signal that thou hear'st something approach.**
11	**Give me those flowers, do as I bid thee, go.**
12	**PAGE:** **I am almost afraid to stand alone**
13	**Here in the churchyard, yet I will adventure.** *(PAGE retires.*
14	*PARIS strews the tomb with flowers.)*
15	**PARIS:** **Sweet flow'r, with flow'rs thy bridal bed I strew.**
16	**O woe, thy canopy is dust and stones.**
17	**Which with sweet water nightly I will dew,**
18	**Or wanting that, with tears distill'd by moans.**
19	**The obsequies that I for thee will keep**
20	**Nightly shall be to strew thy grave and weep.** *(PAGE*
21	*whistles.)*
22	**The boy gives warning something doth approach.**
23	**What cursed foot wanders this way tonight**
24	**To cross my obsequies and true love's rite?**
25	**What! with a torch? Muffle me, night, awhile.** *(PARIS*
26	*retires. Enter ROMEO and BALTHASAR with a*
27	*torch, a mattock and a crow of iron.)*
28	**ROMEO:** **Give me that mattock and the wrenching iron.**
29	**Hold, take this letter, early in the morning**
30	**See thou deliver it to my lord and father.**
31	**Give me the light. Upon thy life I charge thee,**
32	**Whate'er thou hear'st or see'st, stand all aloof**
33	**And do not interrupt me in my course.**
34	**Why I descend into this bed of Death**
35	**Is partly to behold my lady's face,**

1	But chiefly to take thence from her dead finger
2	A precious ring — a ring that I must use
3	In dear employment. Therefore hence, be gone.
4	But if thou jealous dost return to pry
5	In what I farther shall intend to do,
6	By Heaven I will tear thee joint by joint
7	And strew this hungry churchyard with thy limbs.
8	The time and my intents are savage-wild,
9	More fierce and more inexorable far
10	Than empty tigers or the roaring sea.
11	BALTHASAR: I will be gone sir, and not trouble ye.
12	ROMEO: So shalt thou show me friendship. Take thou that,
13	Live and be prosperous. And farewell, good fellow.
14	BALTHASAR: For all this same I'll hide me hereabout,
15	His looks I fear and his intents I doubt. *(BALTHASAR*
16	*retires.)*
17	ROMEO: Thou detestable maw, thou womb of death,
18	Gorg'd with the dearest morsel of the earth,
19	Thus I enforce thy rotten jaws to open,
20	And in despite I'll cram thee with more food. *(ROMEO*
21	*opens the tomb.)*
22	PARIS: This is that banish'd haughty Montague
23	That murder'd my love's cousin (with which grief
24	It is supposed the fair creature died)
25	And here is come to do some villainous shame
26	To the dead bodies. I will apprehend him.
27	Stop thy unhallow'd toil, vile Montague!
28	Can vengeance be pursu'd further than death?
29	Condemned villain, I do apprehend thee.
30	Obey and go with me, for thou must die.
31	ROMEO: I must indeed and therefore came I hither.
32	Good gentle youth, tempt not a desp'rate man,
33	Fly hence and leave me. Think upon these gone,
34	Let them affright thee. I beseech thee, youth,
35	Put not another sin upon my head

1   By urging me to fury. O be gone!

2   By Heav'n, I love thee better than myself,

3   For I come hither arm'd against myself.

4   Stay not, be gone! live, and hereafter say

5   A mad man's mercy bid thee run away.

6 PARIS: I do defy thy conjuration

7   And apprehend thee for a felon here.

8 ROMEO: Wilt thou provoke me? Then have at thee, boy! *(They*

9   *fight.)*

10 PAGE: O Lord, they fight! I will go call the watch. *(PAGE exits.)*

11 PARIS: O I am slain! If thou be merciful

12   Open the tomb, lay me with Juliet.

13 ROMEO: In faith, I will. Let me peruse this face.

14   Mercutio's kinsman, noble County Paris!

15   What said my man when my betossed soul

16   Did not attend him as we rode? I think

17   He told me Paris should have marry'd Juliet.

18   Said he not so? or did I dream it so?

19   Or am I mad, hearing him talk of Juliet,

20   To think it was so? O give me thy hand,

21   One writ with me in sour Misfortune's book.

22   I'll bury thee in a triumphant grave.

23   A grave? O no, a lanthorn, a slaughter'd youth,

24   For here lies Juliet, and her beauty makes

25   This vault a feasting presence full of light.

26   Death, lie thou there, by a dead man interr'd.

27   How oft when men are at the point of death

28   Have they been merry — which their keepers call

29   A lightning before death. O how may I

30   Call this a lightning? O my love, my wife!

31   Death that hath suck'd the honey of thy breath

32   Hath had no power yet upon thy beauty.

33   Thou art not conquer'd — Beauty's ensign yet

34   Is crimson in thy lips and in thy cheeks,

35   And Death's pale flag is not advanced there.

1   Tybalt, ly'st thou there in thy bloody sheet?
2   O what more favor can I do to thee
3   Than with that hand that cut thy youth in twain
4   To sunder his that was thine enemy?
5   Forgive me, cousin. Ah dear Juliet,
6   Why art thou yet so fair? shall I believe
7   That unsubstantial Death is amorous
8   And that the lean abhorred monster keeps
9   Thee here in dark to be his paramour?
10   For fear of that I still will stay with thee
11   And never from this pallet of dim Night
12   Depart again, here, here will I remain
13   With worms that are thy chambermaids, O here
14   Will I set up my everlasting rest
15   And shake the yoke of inauspicious stars
16   From this world-weary'd flesh. Eyes look your last,
17   Arms take your last embrace, and lips (O you
18   The doors of breath) seal with a righteous kiss
19   A dateless bargain to engrossing Death!
20   Come bitter conduct, come unsav'ry guide,
21   Thou desp'rate pilot, now at once run on
22   The dashing rocks thy seasick weary bark.
23   Here's to my love! O true apothecary,
24   Thy drugs are quick. Thus with a kiss I die. *(ROMEO falls.*
25   *Enter FRIAR with lanthorn, crow and spade.)*
26 FRIAR: Saint Francis be my speed! how oft tonight
27   Have my old feet stumbled at graves. Who's there?
28 BALTHASAR: Here's one, a friend, and one that knows you
29   well.
30 FRIAR: Bliss be upon you. Tell me, good my friend,
31   What torch is yond that vainly lends his light
32   To grubs and eyeless skulls? as I discern,
33   It burneth in the Capels' monument.
34 BALTHASAR: It doth so, holy sir, and there's my master,
35   One that you love.

1   **FRIAR:**   Who is it?
2   **BALTHASAR:**   Romeo.
3   **FRIAR:**   How long hath he been there?
4   **BALTHASAR:**   Full half an hour.
5   **FRIAR:**   Go with me to the vault.
6   **BALTHASAR:**   I dare not, sir,
7   My master knows not but I am gone hence,
8   And fearfully did menace me with death
9   If I did stay to look on his intents.
10   **FRIAR:**   Stay then, I'll go alone. Fear comes upon me,
11   O much I fear some ill unthrifty thing.
12   **BALTHASAR:**   As I did sleep under this yew tree here
13   I dreamt my master and another fought
14   And that my master slew him. *(Exit BALTHASAR)*
15   **FRIAR:**   Romeo! *(FRIAR stoops and looks on the blood and*
16   *weapons.)*
17   Alack, alack, what blood is this which stains
18   The stony entrance of this sepulcher?
19   What mean these masterless and gory swords
20   To lie discolor'd by this place of peace?
21   Romeo, O pale! Who else? What! Paris too?
22   And steep'd in blood? Ah what an unkind hour
23   Is guilty of this lamentable chance.
24   The lady stirs. *(JULIET rises.)*
25   **JULIET:**   O comfortable Friar, where is my lord?
26   I do remember well where I should be
27   And there I am, where is my Romeo?
28   **FRIAR:**   I hear some noise, lady, come from that nest
29   Of death, contagion and unnatural sleep.
30   A greater power than we can contradict
31   Hath thwarted our intents, come, come away.
32   Thy husband in thy bosom there lies dead,
33   And Paris too. Come, I'll dispose of thee
34   Among a sisterhood of holy nuns.
35   Stay not to question, for the watch is coming.

1   Come go, good Juliet, I dare no longer stay. *(Exit FRIAR)*
2   JULIET: Go get thee hence, for I will not away.
3   What's here? a cup clos'd in my true love's hand!
4   Poison I see hath been his timeless end.
5   O churl, drunk all and left no friendly drop
6   To help me after? I will kiss thy lips,
7   Haply some poison yet doth hang on them
8   To make me die with a restorative.
9   Thy lips are warm. *(Enter PAGE and CHIEF WATCHMAN)*
10 CHIEF WATCHMAN: Lead boy, which way?
11 JULIET: Yea noise? then I'll be brief. O happy dagger,
12   This is thy sheath — there rust and let me die. *(She stabs*
13   *herself and falls.)*
14
15
16
17
18
19
20
21
22
23
24
25
26
27
28
29
30
31
32
33
34
35

CHARACTERS

Portia — a fair young woman possessing a sharp satiric wit

Nerissa — her closest friend

This scene allows us to truly see the intelligence and wit of Portia. Here is her dilemma: according to the will of her late father, she cannot marry a man of her own choosing. Instead, she must make herself available to all young men and accept the one who chooses "rightly" from among "three chests of gold, silver, and lead." Nerissa, her closest friend, comforts her by trying to convince her that her father's plan must be foolproof; whoever the man might be who finally chooses "rightly" will surely be the "one who shall rightly love."

Nerissa asks Portia about the men who have come to woo her. With sarcastic humor, Portia replies on the faults of each, for none of her suitors interest her; they are either dull, superficial, or drunk. Furthermore, none of the men court her for any length of time because the penalty for choosing the wrong casket condemns each to remain a bachelor for the rest of his life.

Basically, there are three purposes to this scene: 1) to establish the powerful character and wit of Portia; 2) to provide Portia's dilemma, i.e., her father's plan of having her suitors choose from the caskets of gold, silver, or lead; and 3) to introduce (at the end of the scene) Bassanio, the "Venetian scholar and soldier" who will, later in the play, win her heart.

1   *SETTING:*   Portia's house at Belmont.
2   *AT RISE:*   Enter Portia with her waiting woman, Nerissa.
3
4   PORTIA: By my troth, Nerissa, my little body is aweary of
5   this great world.
6   NERISSA: You would be, sweet madam, if your miseries were
7   in the same abundance as your good fortunes are; and
8   yet, for aught I see, they are as sick that surfeit with too
9   much as they that starve with nothing. It is no mean
10   happiness, therefore, to be seated in the mean. Superfluity
11   comes sooner by white hairs, but competency lives longer.
12   PORTIA: Good sentences, and well pronounced.
13   NERISSA: They would be better if well followed.
14   PORTIA: If to do were as easy as to know what were good
15   to do, chapels had been churches, and poor men's cottages
16   princes' palaces. It is a good divine that follows his own
17   instructions. I can easier teach twenty what were good to
18   be done than be one of the twenty to follow mine own
19   teaching. The brain may devise laws for the blood, but a
20   hot temper leaps o'er a cold decree: such a hare is madness
21   the youth, to skip o'er the meshes of good counsel the
22   cripple. But this reasoning is not in the fashion to choose
23   me a husband. O me, the word "choose"! I may neither
24   choose who I would nor refuse who I dislike, so is the will
25   of a living daughter curbed by the will of a dead father.
26   Is it not hard, Nerissa, that I cannot choose one nor refuse
27   none?
28   NERISSA: Your father was ever virtuous, and holy men at
29   their death have good inspirations: therefore the lott'ry
30   that he hath devised in these three chests of gold, silver,
31   and lead, whereof who chooses his meaning chooses you,
32   will no doubt never be chosen by any rightly but one who
33   you shall rightly love. But what warmth is there in your
34   affection towards any of these princely suitors that are
35   already come?

1 PORTIA: I pray thee overname them; and as thou namest
2   them, I will describe them; and according to my
3   description level at my affection.
4 NERISSA: First, there is the Neapolitan prince.
5 PORTIA: Ay, that's a colt indeed, for he doth nothing but talk
6   of his horse, and he makes it a great appropriation unto
7   his own good parts that he can shoe him himself: I am
8   much afeard my lady his mother played false with a smith.
9 NERISSA: Then is there the County Palatine.
10 PORTIA: He doth nothing but frown, as who should say, "An
11   you will not have me, choose!" He hears merry tales and
12   smiles not. I fear he will prove the weeping philosopher
13   when he grows old, being so full of unmannerly sadness
14   in his youth. I had rather be married to a death's-head
15   with a bone in his mouth than to either of these. God defend
16   me from these two!
17 NERISSA: How say you by the French lord, Monsieur Le Bon?
18 PORTIA: God made him, and therefore let him pass for a man.
19   In truth, I know it is a sin to be a mocker, but he — why
20   he hath a horse better than the Neapolitan's, a better bad
21   habit of frowning than the Count Palatine. He is every
22   man in no man. If a throstle sing, he falls straight a-
23   cap'ring; he will fence with his own shadow. If I should
24   marry him, I should marry twenty husbands. If he would
25   despise me, I would forgive him; for if he love me to
26   madness, I shall never requite him.
27 NERISSA: What say you then to Falconbridge, the young
28   baron of England?
29 PORTIA: You know I say nothing to him, for he understands
30   not me, nor I him. He hath neither Latin, French, nor
31   Italian; and you will come into the court and swear that
32   I have a poor pennyworth in the English. He is a proper
33   man's picture, but alas! who can converse with a dumb
34   show? How oddly he is suited! I think he bought his doublet
35   in Italy, his round hose in France, his bonnet in Germany,

1　and his behavior everywhere.

2　NERISSA:　What think you of the Scottish lord, his neighbor?

3　PORTIA:　That he hath a neighborly charity in him, for he

4　　　borrowed a box of the ear of the Englishman, and swore

5　　　he would pay him again when he was able. I think the

6　　　Frenchman became his surety and sealed under for

7　　　another.

8　NERISSA:　How like you the young German, the Duke of

9　　　Saxony's nephew?

10　PORTIA:　Very vilely in the morning when he is sober, and

11　　　most vilely in the afternoon when he is drunk. When he

12　　　is best, he is a little worse than a man, and when he is

13　　　worst, he is little better than a beast: an the worst fall that

14　　　ever fell, I hope I shall make shift to go without him.

15　NERISSA:　If he should offer to choose, and choose the right

16　　　casket, you should refuse to perform your father's will if

17　　　you should refuse to accept him.

18　PORTIA:　Therefore, for fear of the worst, I pray thee set a

19　　　deep glass of Rhenish wine on the contrary casket, for if

20　　　the devil be within and that temptation without, I know

21　　　he will choose it. I will do anything, Nerissa, ere I will be

22　　　married to a sponge.

23　NERISSA:　You need not fear, lady, the having any of these

24　　　lords. They have acquainted me with their determinations,

25　　　which is indeed to return to their home, and to trouble

26　　　you with no more suit, unless you may be won by some

27　　　other sort than your father's imposition, depending on the

28　　　caskets.

29　PORTIA:　If I live to be as old as Sibylla, I will die as chaste

30　　　as Diana unless I be obtained by the manner of my father's

31　　　will. I am glad this parcel of wooers are so reasonable, for

32　　　there is not one among them but I dote on his very absence;

33　　　and I pray God grant them a fair departure.

34　NERISSA:　Do you not remember, lady, in your father's time,

35　　　a Venetian, a scholar and a soldier, that came hither in

1   company of the Marquis of Montferrat?
2 PORTIA: Yes, yes, it was Bassanio, as I think, so was he called.
3
4
5
6
7
8
9
10
11
12
13
14
15
16
17
18
19
20
21
22
23
24
25
26
27
28
29
30
31
32
33
34
35

CHARACTERS

Bassanio — a young man from Venice who is seeking a loan from Shylock

Antonio — Bassanio's wealthy friend

Shylock — a Jewish moneylender

Bassanio seeks out Shylock for a loan of three thousand ducats. His friend, Antonio, is wealthy but, at the moment, has his money invested in his merchant fleet which is currently out to sea. Antonio does, however, lend his good name and promise to Shylock, thus giving more credit to Bassanio.

However, Shylock hates Antonio not only because he is a Christian, but, more importantly, he hates Antonio because Antonio lends money to people without charging interest; moreover, Antonio publicly condemns Shylock for charging excessive interest in his moneylending business.

It is important to capture the true character of Shylock: at first, he almost feels badgered, like an adult being pestered by an impatient child, then he seems to digress, avoiding answering straightforwardly. Furthermore, audiences are quick to label him a villain because he hates a man for simply being a Christian; however, in his speech we realize the depth and complexity of his situation and are given a most revealing glimpse of a man who has been a victim.

While Bassanio and Antonio are waiting to learn the rate of interest Shylock will charge them for the loan, they become impatient while Shylock tells them a biblical story. Shylock suddenly accuses Antonio of spitting on him and calling him a dog . . . and now has the nerve to come and ask him for money. Antonio states that this is not to be regarded as a loan between friends; surprisingly, Shylock says he wants Antonio's friendship, and to prove it, he will grant the loan and not charge a penny of interest.

He does, however, want a penalty clause providing that if Antonio fails to repay the loan within the three-month period, Shylock will have the right to cut "a pound of flesh" from any part of Antonio's body. With some protest from Bassanio, Antonio agrees to Shylock's terms.

1   *SETTING:*   A street in Venice.
2   *AT RISE:*   Enter Bassanio with Shylock the Jew.
3
4   SHYLOCK: Three thousand ducats — well.
5   BASSANIO: Ay, sir, for three months.
6   SHYLOCK: For three months — well.
7   BASSANIO: For the which, as I told you, Antonio shall be
8   bound.
9   SHYLOCK: Antonio shall become bound — well.
10   BASSANIO: May you stead me? Will you pleasure me? Shall
11   I know your answer?
12   SHYLOCK: Three thousand ducats for three months, and
13   Antonio bound.
14   BASSANIO: Your answer to that.
15   SHYLOCK: Antonio is a good man.
16   BASSANIO: Have you heard any imputation to the contrary?
17   SHYLOCK: Ho, no, no, no, no! My meaning in saying he is a
18   good man is to have you understand me that he is sufficient.
19   Yet his means are in supposition: he hath an argosy bound
20   to Tripolis, another to the Indies. I understand, moreover,
21   upon the Rialto, he hath a third at Mexico, a fourth for
22   England, and other ventures he hath, squand'red abroad.
23   But ships are but boards, sailors but men; there be land
24   rats and water rats, water thieves and land thieves — I
25   mean pirates; and then there is the peril of waters, winds,
26   and rocks — the man is, notwithstanding, sufficient —
27   three thousand ducats — I think I may take his bond.
28   BASSANIO: Be assured you may.
29   SHYLOCK: I will be assured I may; and that I may be assured,
30   I will bethink me. May I speak with Antonio?
31   BASSANIO: If it please you to dine with us.
32   SHYLOCK: Yes, to smell pork, to eat of the habitation which
33   your prophet the Nazarite conjured the devil into! I will
34   buy with you, sell with you, talk with you, walk with you,
35   and so following; but I will not eat with you, drink with

1   you, nor pray with you. What news on the Rialto? Who is
2   he comes here? *(Enter ANTONIO)*
3   BASSANIO: This is Signior Antonio.
4   SHYLOCK: *(Aside)* How like a fawning publican he looks!
5   I hate him for he is a Christian;
6   But more for that in low simplicity
7   He lends out money gratis and brings down
8   The rate of usance here with us in Venice.
9   If I can catch him once upon the hip,
10   I will feed fat the ancient grudge I bear him.
11   He hates our sacred nation, and he rails,
12   Even there where merchants most do congregate,
13   On me, my bargains, and my well-won thrift,
14   Which he calls interest. Cursed be my tribe
15   If I forgive him!
16 BASSANIO: Shylock, do you hear?
17 SHYLOCK: I am debating of my present store,
18   And by the near guess of my memory
19   I cannot instantly raise up the gross
20   Of full three thousand ducats. What of that?
21   Tubal, a wealthy Hebrew of my tribe,
22   Will furnish me. But soft! How many months
23   Do you desire? — *(To ANTONIO)* Rest you fair, good
24   signior!
25   Your worship was the last man in our mouths.
26 ANTONIO: Shylock, albeit I neither lend nor borrow
27   By taking nor by giving of excess,
28   Yet, to supply the ripe wants of my friend,
29   I'll break a custom. *(To BASSANIO)* Is he yet possessed
30   How much ye would?
31 SHYLOCK: Ay, ay, three thousand ducats.
32 ANTONIO: And for three months.
33 SHYLOCK: I had forgot — three months, you told me so.
34   Well then, your bond. And let me see — but hear you:
35   Methoughts you said you neither lend nor borrow

1   Upon advantage.
2   ANTONIO: I do never use it.
3   SHYLOCK: When Jacob grazed his uncle Laban's sheep —
4   This Jacob from our holy Abram was
5   (As his wise mother wrought in his behalf)
6   The third possessor; ay, he was the third —
7   ANTONIO: And what of him? Did he take interest?
8   SHYLOCK: No, not take interest; not, as you would say,
9   Directly int'rest. Mark what Jacob did.
10   When Laban and himself were compromised
11   That all the eanlings which were streaked and pied
12   Should fall as Jacob's hire, the ewes, being rank,
13   In end of autumn turned to the rams,
14   And when the work of generation was
15   Between these woolly breeders in the act,
16   The skilful shepherd pilled me certain wands,
17   And, in the doing of the deed of kind,
18   He stuck them up before the fulsome ewes,
19   Who then conceiving, did in eaning time
20   Fall parti-colored lambs, and those were Jacob's.
21   This was a way to thrive, and he was blest;
22   And thrift is blessing, if men steal it not.
23   ANTONIO: This was a venture, sir, that Jacob served for,
24   A thing not in his power to bring to pass,
25   But swayed and fashioned by the hand of heaven.
26   Was this inserted to make interest good?
27   Or is your gold and silver ewes and rams?
28   SHYLOCK: I cannot tell, I make it breed as fast —
29   But note me, signior.
30   ANTONIO: *(Aside)* Mark you this, Bassanio,
31   The devil can cite Scripture for his purpose.
32   An evil soul, producing holy witness,
33   Is like a villain with a smiling cheek,
34   A goodly apple rotten at the heart.
35   O, what a goodly outside falsehood hath!

1   SHYLOCK: Three thousand ducats — 'tis a good round sum.

2   Three months from twelve — then, let me see, the rate —

3   ANTONIO: Well, Shylock, shall we be beholding to you?

4   SHYLOCK: Signior Antonio, many a time and oft

5   In the Rialto you have rated me

6   About my moneys and my usances:

7   Still have I borne it with a patient shrug,

8   For suff'rance is the badge of all our tribe.

9   You call me misbeliever, cutthroat dog,

10   And spet upon my Jewish gaberdine,

11   And all for use of that which is mine own.

12   Well then, it now appears you need my help:

13   Go to then, you come to me and you say,

14   "Shylock, we would have moneys." You say so —

15   You that did void your rheum upon my beard

16   And foot me as you spurn a stranger cur

17   Over your threshold. Moneys is your suit.

18   What should I say to you? Should I not say,

19   "Hath a dog money? Is it possible

20   A cur can lend three thousand ducats?" or

21   Shall I bend low, and in a bondman's key,

22   With bated breath and whisp'ring humbleness,

23   Say this:

24   "Fair sir, you spet on me on Wednesday last;

25   You spurned me such a day; another time

26   You called me dog; and for these courtesies

27   I'll lend you thus much moneys"?

28   ANTONIO: I am as like to call thee so again,

29   To spet on thee again, to spurn thee too.

30   If thou wilt lend this money, lend it not

31   As to thy friends, for when did friendship take

32   A breed for barren metal of his friend?

33   But lend it rather to thine enemy,

34   Who if he break, thou mayst with better face

35   Exact the penalty.

1   SHYLOCK: Why, look you, how you storm!
2   I would be friends with you and have your love,
3   Forget the shames that you have stained me with,
4   Supply your present wants, and take no doit
5   Of usance for my moneys,
6   And you'll not hear me. This is kind I offer.
7   BASSANIO: This were kindness.
8   SHYLOCK: This kindness will I show.
9   Go with me to a notary, seal me there
10   Your single bond; and, in a merry sport,
11   If you repay me not on such a day,
12   In such a place, such sum or sums as are
13   Expressed in the condition, let the forfeit
14   Be nominated for an equal pound
15   Of your fair flesh, to be cut off and taken
16   In what part of your body pleaseth me.
17   ANTONIO: Content, in faith. I'll seal to such a bond,
18   And say there is much kindness in the Jew.
19   BASSANIO: You shall not seal to such a bond for me!
20   I'll rather dwell in my necessity.
21   ANTONIO: Why, fear not, man! I will not forfeit it.
22   Within these two months — that's a month before
23   This bond expires — I do expect return
24   Of thrice three times the value of this bond.
25   SHYLOCK: O father Abram, what these Christians are,
26   Whose own hard dealing teaches them suspect
27   The thoughts of others! Pray you tell me this:
28   If he should break his day, what should I gain
29   By the exaction of the forfeiture?
30   A pound of man's flesh taken from a man
31   Is not so estimable, profitable neither,
32   As flesh of muttons, beefs, or goats. I say,
33   To buy his favor I extend this friendship.
34   If he will take it, so; if not, adieu;
35   And for my love I pray you wrong me not.

1   ANTONIO: Yes, Shylock, I will seal unto this bond.
2   SHYLOCK: Then meet me forthwith at the notary's;
3   Give him direction for this merry bond,
4   And I will go and purse the ducats straight,
5   See to my house, left in the fearful guard
6   Of an unthrifty knave, and presently
7   I will be with you.
8   ANTONIO: Hie thee, gentle Jew. *(Exit SHYLOCK)*
9   The Hebrew will turn Christian; he grows kind.
10   BASSANIO: I like not fair terms and a villain's mind.
11   ANTONIO: Come on, in this there can be no dismay;
12   My ships come home a month before the day. *(Exit*
13   *BASSANIO and ANTONIO)*
14
15
16
17
18
19
20
21
22
23
24
25
26
27
28
29
30
31
32
33
34
35

MAJOR CHARACTERS

Caesar — the ruler of Rome. He is a successful political leader and very popular with Roman citizens. However, there is a small band of conspirators who find him too "ambitious."

Calpurnia — his loyal and faithful wife

Decius — a member of the conspiracy; he is sent to bring Caesar to the Capitol, where he and other members of the conspiracy shall assassinate him. Decius is clever, and he knows that Caesar responds to flattery.

MINOR CHARACTER — Servant of Caesar

EXTRAS — Publius, Trebonius, and other conspirators

To fully understand the characters' motivations in this scene, we must return to the play's beginnings. Before 509 B.C., Rome was ruled by a monarchy, but in that year the citizens, led by the Brutus family, overthrew the existing leadership and established a republic. However, there still remained a large gap between the common people, or plebeians, and the wealthy ruling class, or patricians.

By Julius Caesar's lifetime (100-44 B.C.), Rome was a moderate democracy, but government officials were engaged in personal rivalries.

By serving in various offices, Caesar, a patrician, became very popular with the common people. He spent tax dollars on public entertainment and established laws to free farmers, tradesmen, and small businessmen from devastating taxes and debts.

In 60 B.C. he formed, with Crassus and Pompey, a triumvirate (three-man rule). Caesar's popularity continued to grow: he became governor of Gaul, province of Rome, and went on to conquer the rest of Gaul, funneling large amounts of money into the Roman Empire.

However, the triumvirate was short-lived. Crassus was slain in Mesopotamia, and Pompey became more and more jealous of Caesar. As a matter of fact, he alarmed senators of Caesar's growth in power and convinced them to order him to disband his army or be considered an enemy of Rome. Caesar met this challenge and led his army into Rome and became ruler of the Roman world.

He was made dictator in 48 B.C.; in 46 B.C. he was named dictator for 10 years; in 45 B.C. he was named dictator for life.

When the play begins, Caesar is returning from a successful campaign in Spain. However, there is a small group of leading citizens who feel that Caesar has become too powerful and ambitious. Led by Cassius, these men need an honest and respected citizen to join their conspiracy to give it merit. They plan to assassinate Caesar in the Capitol in broad daylight — with an honest man like Brutus involved, they hope the Roman citizens will believe the killing was done for the betterment of Rome.

The conspiracy convinces Brutus to join their cause. On the morning of the planned assassination, the Ides of March, they send fellow conspirator, Decius, to bring Caesar to the Capitol.

As this scene opens, it is important to note that Caesar not only believed in fatalism ("What can be avoided whose end is purposed by the mighty gods?"), but he is influenced by Calpurnia's nightmare, which she interprets as a foreshadow of Caesar's death.

Just as Caesar agrees to stay home from the Capitol, Decius arrives, re-interprets the dream, and, flattering Caesar, leads him to the Capitol and to his death.

1   **SETTING:**   Caesar's house
2   **AT RISE:**   Thunder and lightning. Enter Julius Caesar in his
3   nightgown.
4
5   CAESAR: Nor heaven nor earth have been at peace tonight:
6   Thrice hath Calpurnia in her sleep cried out,
7   "Help, ho! They murder Caesar!" Who's within? *(Enter a*
8   *SERVANT)*
9   SERVANT: My lord!
10   CAESAR: Go bid the priests do present sacrifice,
11   And bring me their opinions of success.
12   SERVANT: I will, my lord. *(He exits. Enter CALPURNIA)*
13   CALPURNIA: What mean you, Caesar? Think you to walk
14   forth?
15   You shall not stir out of your house today.
16   CAESAR: Caesar shall forth: the things that threaten'd me
17   Ne'er look'd but on my back; when they shall see
18   The face of Caesar, they are vanished.
19   CALPURNIA: Caesar, I never stood on ceremonies,
20   Yet now they fright me. There is one within,
21   Besides the things that we have heard and seen,
22   Recounts most horrid sights seen by the watch.
23   A lioness hath whelped in the streets;
24   And graves have yawn'd and yielded up their dead;
25   Fierce fiery warriors fought upon the clouds,
26   In ranks and squadrons and right form of war,
27   Which drizzled blood upon the Capitol;
28   The noise of battle hurtled in the air,
29   Horses did neigh, and dying men did groan,
30   And ghosts did shriek and squeal about the streets.
31   O Caesar, these things are beyond all use,
32   And I do fear them.
33   CAESAR: What can be avoided
34   Whose end is purpos'd by the mighty gods?
35   Yet Caesar shall go forth; for these predictions

1   Are to the world in general as to Caesar.
2 CALPURNIA: When beggars die there are no comets seen;
3   The heavens themselves blaze forth the death of princes.
4 CAESAR: Cowards die many times before their deaths;
5   The valiant never taste of death but once.
6   Of all the wonders that I yet have heard,
7   It seems to me most strange that men should fear;
8   Seeing that death, a necessary end,
9   Will come when it will come. *(Enter a SERVANT)* What say
10   the augurers?
11 SERVANT: They would not have you to stir forth today.
12   Plucking the entrails of an offering forth,
13   They could not find a heart within the beast.
14 CAESAR: The gods do this in shame of cowardice:
15   Caesar should be a beast without a heart
16   If he should stay at home today for fear.
17   No, Caesar shall not; danger knows full well
18   That Caesar is more dangerous than he:
19   We are two lions litter'd in one day,
20   And I the elder and more terrible:
21   And Caesar shall go forth.
22 CALPURNIA: Alas, my lord,
23   Your wisdom is consum'd in confidence.
24   Do not go forth today: call it my fear
25   That keeps you in the house, and not your own.
26   We'll send Mark Antony to the senate-house,
27   And he shall say you are not well today:
28   Let me, upon my knee, prevail in this.
29 CAESAR: Mark Antony shall say I am not well;
30   And, for thy humor, I will stay at home. *(Enter DECIUS)*
31   Here's Decius Brutus, he shall tell them so.
32 DECIUS: Caesar, all hail! Good morrow, worthy Caesar:
33   I come to fetch you to the senate-house.
34 CAESAR: And you are come in very happy time
35   To bear my greeting to the senators,

1   And tell them that I will not come today:

2   Cannot, is false, and that I dare not, falser;

3   I will not come today: tell them so, Decius.

4 CALPURNIA: Say he is sick.

5 CAESAR: Shall Caesar send a lie?

6   Have I in conquest stretch'd mine arm so far

7   To be afeard to tell greybeards the truth?

8   Decius, go tell them Caesar will not come.

9 DECIUS: Most mighty Caesar, let me know some cause,

10   Lest I be laugh'd at when I tell them so.

11 CAESAR: The cause is in my will: I will not come;

12   That is enough to satisfy the senate:

13   But for your private satisfaction,

14   Because I love you, I will let you know:

15   Calpurnia here, my wife, stays me at home:

16   She dreamt tonight she saw my statue,

17   Which, like a fountain with a hundred spouts,

18   Did run pure blood; and many lusty Romans

19   Came smiling, and did bathe their hands in it:

20   And these does she apply for warnings and portents,

21   And evils imminent; and on her knee

22   Hath begg'd that I will stay at home today.

23 DECIUS: This dream is all amiss interpreted;

24   It was a vision fair and fortunate:

25   Your statue spouting blood in many pipes,

26   In which so many smiling Romans bath'd,

27   Signifies that from you great Rome shall suck

28   Reviving blood, and that great men shall press

29   For tinctures, stains, relics, and cognizance.

30   This by Calpurnia's dream is signified.

31 CAESAR: And this way have you well expounded it.

32 DECIUS: I have, when you have heard what I can say;

33   And know it now: the senate have concluded

34   To give this day a crown to mighty Caesar.

35   If you shall send them word you will not come,

1   Their minds may change. Besides, it were a mock

2   Apt to be render'd, for someone to say,

3   "Break up the senate till another time,

4   When Caesar's wife shall meet with better dreams."

5   If Caesar hide himself, shall they not whisper,

6   "Lo, Caesar is afraid"?

7   Pardon me, Caesar; for my dear dear love

8   To your proceeding bids me tell you this,

9   And reason to my love is liable.

10   CAESAR: How foolish do your fears seem now, Calpurnia!

11   I am ashamed I did yield to them.

12   Give me my robe, for I will go. *(Enter BRUTUS, LIGARIUS,*

13   *METELLUS, CASCA, TREBONIUS, CINNA, and*

14   *PUBLIUS.)*

15   And look where Publius is come to fetch me.

16   PUBLIUS: Good morrow, Caesar.

17   CAESAR: Welcome, Publius.

18   What, Brutus, are you stirr'd so early too?

19   Good morrow, Casca. Caius Ligarius,

20   Caesar was ne'er so much your enemy

21   As that same ague which hath made you lean.

22   What is't o'clock?

23   BRUTUS: Caesar, 'tis strucken eight.

24   CAESAR: I thank you for your pains and courtesy. *(Enter*

25   *ANTONY)*

26   See, Antony, that revels long o' nights,

27   Is notwithstanding up. Good morrow, Antony.

28   ANTONY: So to most noble Caesar.

29   CAESAR: Bid them prepare within:

30   I am to blame to be thus waited for.

31   Now, Cinna; now, Metellus; what, Trebonius,

32   I have an hour's talk in store for you;

33   Remember that you call on me today:

34   Be near me, that I may remember you.

35   TREBONIUS: *(Aside)* and so near will I be,

1   That your best friends shall wish I had been further.
2 CAESAR: Good friends, go in, and taste some wine with me;
3   And we, like friends, will straightway go together.
4 BRUTUS: *(Aside)* That every "like" is not "the same," O
5   Caesar,
6   The heart of Brutus yearns to think upon. *(All exit.)*
7
8
9
10
11
12
13
14
15
16
17
18
19
20
21
22
23
24
25
26
27
28
29
30
31
32
33
34
35

Julius Caesar
Act III, Scene 2

MAJOR CHARACTERS

Brutus — considered to be the "noblest Roman of them all." Earlier in the play, he is approached by a band of conspirators to assassinate Caesar for the good of Rome.

Antony — Caesar's closest and most loyal friend. He is a great speaker and utilizes subtleties and emotional ploys to sway the populace to turn against the conspirators.

EXTRAS — Citizens

This scene is one of the most memorable in all of Shakespeare's works: it demonstrates how a crowd, or mob, if you will, can be swayed and influenced by a great speaker.

Here is what has occurred thus far: Caesar has just returned from a successful campaign in Spain as the play begins. (For further information on the events preceding his return, please refer to the description on page 39, Julius Caesar, Act II, Scene 2.) There is a band of leading citizens who fear Caesar's growth in power and form a conspiracy whose goal is to assassinate him. However, to insure merit to their plan, they convince Brutus, a highly respected Roman, to join their cause. They believe, therefore, that the citizens will think that the assassination is justified; after all, Brutus is respected and loved and will do nothing to harm the Roman cause.

This scene takes place immediately after the assassination. The stunned crowd who has witnessed Caesar's death becomes angry and unruly, demanding an explanation for this catastrophic event. Brutus goes to the pulpit first to speak to the crowd, explaining that he killed him "not that I loved Caesar less, but that I loved Rome more." As Brutus speaks, he persuades the crowd in believing that the murder was justified. He then allows Antony, Caesar's close friend, to speak. This is one of two fatal mistakes Brutus makes: the first mistake was to let Antony live; they discussed killing Antony along with Caesar, but Brutus thought the citizens would think "the course too bloody."

Antony then speaks. As he begins, he knows that he is facing a hostile crowd, so he must proceed carefully. However, as he continues, his confidence rises as he senses the crowd reacting to his speech. Please make special note of the subtle tools that Antony uses to sway the crowd to his favor: the tears, the reading of the will, the display of the bloody corpse.

This scene could be an excellent devise to use to introduce a Shakespearian unit in an acting class. The instructor (or a strong actor) can read the part of Antony, and four group leaders can read the lines of the citizens; furthermore, the entire class may react to what is being said, but they must learn when to react and whether their reaction at a particular point is hostile, neutral, or supportive.

The crowd leaders can speak all the lines from the play, and the members of the group may echo the leader's comments or shout their own approval or disapproval, suiting their actions to their words.

1   *SETTING:*   The Forum

2   *AT RISE:*   Enter Brutus and presently goes into the pulpit, and

3   Cassius with the Plebeians.

4

5   PLEBEIANS: We will be satisfied: let us be satisfied.

6   BRUTUS: Then follow me, and give me audience, friends.

7   Cassius, go you into the other street,

8   And part the numbers.

9   Those that will hear me speak, let 'em stay here;

10   Those that will follow Cassius, go with him;

11   And public reasons shall be rendered

12   Of Caesar's death.

13   FIRST PLEBEIAN: I will hear Brutus speak.

14   SECOND PLEBEIAN: I will hear Cassius, and compare their

15   reasons,

16   When severally we hear them rendered. *(Exit CASSIUS*

17   *with some of the PLEBEIANS)*

18   THIRD PLEBEIAN: The noble Brutus is ascended: silence!

19   BRUTUS: Be patient till the last.

20   Romans, countrymen, and lovers, hear me for my cause,

21   and be silent, that you may hear: believe me for mine

22   honor, and have respect to mine honor, that you may

23   believe: censure me in your wisdom, and awake your

24   senses, that you may the better judge. If there be any in

25   this assembly, any dear friend of Caesar's, to him I say,

26   that Brutus' love to Caesar was no less than his. If then

27   that friend demand why Brutus rose against Caesar, this

28   is my answer: Not that I loved Caesar less, but that I loved

29   Rome more. Had you rather Caesar were living, and die

30   all slaves, than that Caesar were dead, to live all free men?

31   As Caesar loved me, I weep for him; as he was fortunate,

32   I rejoice at it; as he was valiant, I honor him; but, as he

33   was ambitious, I slew him. There is tears, for his love; joy,

34   for his fortune; honor, for his valor; and death, for his

35   ambition. Who is here so base that would be a bondman?

1   If any, speak; for him have I offended. Who is here so rude

2   that would not be a Roman? If any, speak; for him have I

3   offended. Who is here so vile that will not love his country?

4   If any, speak; for him have I offended. I pause for a reply.

5 ALL: None, Brutus, none.

6 BRUTUS: Then none have I offended. I have done no more

7   to Caesar, than you shall do to Brutus. The question of

8   his death is enrolled in the Capitol; his glory not

9   extenuated, wherein he was worthy, nor his offences

10   enforced, for which he suffered death. *(Enter MARK*

11   *ANTONY, with Caesar's body.)* Here comes his body,

12   mourned by Mark Antony: who, though he had no hand

13   in his death, shall receive the benefit of his dying, a place

14   in the commonwealth; as which of you shall not? With this

15   I depart: that, as I slew my best lover for the good of Rome,

16   I have the same dagger for myself, when it shall please

17   my country to need my death.

18 ALL: Live, Brutus! live! live!

19 FIRST PLEBEIAN: Bring him with triumph home unto his

20   house.

21 SECOND PLEBEIAN: Give him a statue with his ancestors.

22 THIRD PLEBEIAN: Let him be Caesar.

23 FOURTH PLEBEIAN: Caesar's better parts

24   Shall be crown'd in Brutus.

25 FIRST PLEBEIAN: We'll bring him to his house with shouts

26   and clamors.

27 BRUTUS: My countrymen, —

28 SECOND PLEBEIAN: Peace! silence! Brutus speaks.

29 FIRST PLEBEIAN: Peace, ho!

30 BRUTUS: Good countrymen, let me depart alone,

31   And, for my sake, stay here with Antony.

32   Do grace to Caesar's corpse, and grace his speech

33   Tending to Caesar's glories, which Mark Antony,

34   By our permission, is allow'd to make.

35   I do entreat you, not a man depart,

1   Save I alone, till Antony have spoke. *(Exit BRUTUS)*

2   FIRST PLEBEIAN: Stay, ho! and let us hear Mark Antony.

3   THIRD PLEBEIAN: Let him go up into the public chair;

4   We'll hear him. Noble Antony, go up.

5   ANTONY: For Brutus' sake, I am beholding to you. *(ANTONY*

6   *goes up.)*

7   FOURTH PLEBEIAN: What does he say of Brutus?

8   THIRD PLEBEIAN: He says, for Brutus' sake,

9   He finds himself beholding to us all.

10   FOURTH PLEBEIAN: 'Twere best he speak no harm of

11   Brutus here.

12   FIRST PLEBEIAN: This Caesar was a tyrant.

13   THIRD PLEBEIAN: Nay, that's certain:

14   We are bless'd that Rome is rid of him.

15   SECOND PLEBEIAN: Peace! let us hear what Antony can

16   say.

17   ANTONY: You gentle Romans, —

18   ALL: Peace, ho! let us hear him.

19   ANTONY: Friends, Romans, countrymen, lend me your ears;

20   I come to bury Caesar, not to praise him.

21   The evil that men do lives after them,

22   The good is oft interred with their bones;

23   So let it be with Caesar. The noble Brutus

24   Hath told you Caesar was ambitious;

25   If it were so, it was a grievous fault,

26   And grievously hath Caesar answer'd it.

27   Here, under leave of Brutus and the rest, —

28   For Brutus is an honorable man;

29   So are they all, all honorable men, —

30   Come I to speak in Caesar's funeral.

31   He was my friend, faithful and just to me:

32   But Brutus says he was ambitious;

33   And Brutus is an honorable man.

34   He hath brought many captives home to Rome,

35   Whose ransoms did the general coffers fill:

1   Did this in Caesar seem ambitious?
2   When that the poor have cried, Caesar hath wept;
3   Ambition should be made of sterner stuff:
4   Yet Brutus says he was ambitious;
5   And Brutus is an honorable man.
6   You all did see that on the Lupercal
7   I thrice presented him a kingly crown,
8   Which he did thrice refuse: was this ambition?
9   Yet Brutus says he was ambitious;
10   And, sure, he is an honorable man.
11   I speak not to disprove what Brutus spoke,
12   But here I am to speak what I do know.
13   You all did love him once, not without cause:
14   What cause withholds you then to mourn for him?
15   O judgment, thou art fled to brutish beasts,
16   And men have lost their reason. Bear with me;
17   My heart is in the coffin there with Caesar,
18   And I must pause till it come back to me.
19 FIRST PLEBEIAN: Methinks there is much reason in his
20   sayings.
21 SECOND PLEBEIAN: If thou consider rightly of the matter,
22   Caesar has had great wrong.
23 THIRD PLEBEIAN: Has he, masters?
24   I fear there will a worse come in his place.
25 FOURTH PLEBEIAN: Mark'd ye his words? He would not
26   take the crown;
27   Therefore 'tis certain he was not ambitious.
28 FIRST PLEBEIAN: If it be found so, some will dear abide it.
29 SECOND PLEBEIAN: Poor soul, his eyes are red as fire with
30   weeping.
31 THIRD PLEBEIAN: There's not a nobler man in Rome than
32   Antony.
33 FOURTH PLEBEIAN: Now mark him; he begins again to
34   speak.
35 ANTONY: But yesterday the word of Caesar might

1	Have stood against the world; now lies he there,
2	And none so poor to do him reverence.
3	O masters, if I were dispos'd to stir
4	Your hearts and minds to mutiny and rage,
5	I should do Brutus wrong, and Cassius wrong,
6	Who, you all know, are honorable men.
7	I will not do them wrong; I rather choose
8	To wrong the dead, to wrong myself, and you,
9	Than I will wrong such honorable men.
10	But here's a parchment with the seal of Caesar;
11	I found it in his closet; 'tis his will.
12	Let but the commons hear this testament —
13	Which, pardon me, I do not mean to read —
14	And they would go and kiss dead Caesar's wounds,
15	And dip their napkins in his sacred blood,
16	Yea, beg a hair of him for memory,
17	And, dying, mention it within their wills,
18	Bequeathing it as a rich legacy
19	Unto their issue.
20	FOURTH PLEBEIAN: We'll hear the will: read it, Mark
21	Antony.
22	ALL: The will, the will! we will hear Caesar's will!
23	ANTONY: Have patience, gentle friends; I must not read it:
24	It is not meet you know how Caesar lov'd you.
25	You are not wood, you are not stones, but men:
26	And, being men, hearing the will of Caesar,
27	It will inflame you, it will make you mad.
28	'Tis good you know not that you are his heirs;
29	For if you should, O what would come of it?
30	FOURTH PLEBEIAN: Read the will! we'll hear it, Antony.
31	You shall read us the will, Caesar's will.
32	ANTONY: Will you be patient? Will you stay awhile?
33	I have o'ershot myself to tell you of it.
34	I fear I wrong the honorable men
35	Whose daggers have stabb'd Caesar; I do fear it.

1   FOURTH PLEBEIAN: They were traitors: honorable men!

2   ALL: The will! the testament!

3   SECOND PLEBEIAN: They were villains, murderers. The

4   will! read the will.

5   ANTONY: You will compel me then to read the will?

6   Then make a ring about the corpse of Caesar,

7   And let me show you him that made the will.

8   Shall I descend? And will you give me leave?

9   ALL: Come down.

10   SECOND PLEBEIAN: Descend.

11   THIRD PLEBEIAN: You shall have leave.

12   FOURTH PLEBEIAN: A ring; stand round.

13   FIRST PLEBEIAN: Stand from the hearse; stand from the

14   body. *(ANTONY comes down.)*

15   SECOND PLEBEIAN: Room for Antony, most noble Antony.

16   ANTONY: Nay, press not so upon me; stand far off.

17   ALL: Stand back! room! bear back!

18   ANTONY: If you have tears, prepare to shed them now.

19   You all do know this mantle: I remember

20   The first time ever Caesar put it on;

21   'Twas on a summer's evening, in his tent,

22   That day he overcame the Nervii.

23   Look, in this place ran Cassius' dagger through:

24   See what a rent the envious Casca made:

25   Through this the well-beloved Brutus stabb'd;

26   And, as he pluck'd his cursed steel away,

27   Mark how the blood of Caesar follow'd it,

28   As rushing out of doors, to be resolv'd

29   If Brutus so unkindly knock'd or no;

30   For Brutus, as you know, was Caesar's angel:

31   Judge, O you gods, how dearly Caesar lov'd him.

32   This was the most unkindest cut of all;

33   For when the noble Caesar saw him stab,

34   Ingratitude, more strong than traitors' arms,

35   Quite vanquish'd him: then burst his mighty heart;

1   And, in his mantle muffling up his face,

2   Even at the base of Pompey's statue,

3   Which all the while ran blood, great Caesar fell.

4   O, what a fall was there, my countrymen!

5   Then I, and you, and all of us fell down,

6   Whilst bloody treason flourish'd over us.

7   O now you weep, and I perceive you feel

8   The dint of pity; these are gracious drops.

9   Kind souls, what, weep you when you but behold

10   Our Caesar's vesture wounded? Look you here,

11   Here is himself, marr'd, as you see, with traitors.

12 FIRST PLEBEIAN: O piteous spectacle!

13 SECOND PLEBEIAN: O noble Caesar!

14 THIRD PLEBEIAN: O woeful day!

15 FOURTH PLEBEIAN: O traitors! villains!

16 FIRST PLEBEIAN: O most bloody sight!

17 SECOND PLEBEIAN: We will be revenged.

18 ALL: Revenge! — About! — Seek! — Burn! — Fire! — Kill!

19   Slay! Let not a traitor live!

20 ANTONY: Stay, countrymen, —

21 FIRST PLEBEIAN: Peace there! Hear the noble Antony.

22 SECOND PLEBEIAN: We'll hear him, we'll follow him, we'll

23   die with him!

24 ANTONY: Good friends, sweet friends, let me not stir you up

25   To such a sudden flood of mutiny.

26   They that have done this deed are honorable:

27   What private griefs they have, alas, I know not,

28   That made them do it; they are wise and honorable,

29   And will, no doubt, with reasons answer you.

30   I come not, friends, to steal away your hearts:

31   I am no orator, as Brutus is;

32   But, as you know me all, a plain blunt man,

33   That love my friend; and that they know full well

34   That gave me public leave to speak of him.

35   For I have neither wit, nor words, nor worth,

1   Action, nor utterance, nor the power of speech,
2   To stir men's blood: I only speak right on;
3   I tell you that which you yourselves do know,
4   Show you sweet Caesar's wounds, poor poor dumb
5   mouths,
6   And bid them speak for me: but were I Brutus,
7   And Brutus Antony, there were an Antony
8   Would ruffle up your spirits, and put a tongue
9   In every wound of Caesar, that should move
10   The stones of Rome to rise and mutiny.
11   ALL: We'll mutiny.
12   FIRST PLEBEIAN: We'll burn the house of Brutus.
13   THIRD PLEBEIAN: Away, then! Come, seek the conspirators.
14   ANTONY: Yet hear me, countrymen; yet hear me speak.
15   ALL: Peace, ho! — Hear Antony, most noble Antony!
16   ANTONY: Why, friends, you go to do you know not what.
17   Wherein hath Caesar thus deserv'd your loves?
18   Alas, you know not: I must tell you then.
19   You have forgot the will I told you of.
20   ALL: Most true. The will! Let's stay and hear the will.
21   ANTONY: Here is the will, and under Caesar's seal.
22   To every Roman citizen he gives,
23   To every several man, seventy-five drachmas.
24   SECOND PLEBEIAN: Most noble Caesar! We'll revenge his
25   death.
26   THIRD PLEBEIAN: O royal Caesar!
27   ANTONY: Hear me with patience.
28   ALL: Peace, ho!
29   ANTONY: Moreover, he hath left you all his walks,
30   His private arbors, and new-planted orchards,
31   On this side Tiber; he hath left them you,
32   And to your heirs for ever; common pleasures,
33   To walk abroad and recreate yourselves.
34   Here was a Caesar! When comes such another?
35   FIRST PLEBEIAN: Never, never! Come, away, away!

1   We'll burn his body in the holy place,
2   And with the brands fire the traitors' houses.
3   Take up the body.
4 SECOND PLEBEIAN: Go fetch fire.
5 THIRD PLEBEIAN: Pluck down benches.
6 FOURTH PLEBEIAN: Pluck down forms, windows,
7   anything. *(Exit PLEBEIANS with the body)*
8 ANTONY: Now let it work: mischief, thou art afoot;
9   Take thou what course thou wilt! *(Enter SERVANT)* How
10   now, fellow!
11 SERVANT: Sir, Octavius is already come to Rome.
12 ANTONY: Where is he?
13 SERVANT: He and Lepidus are at Caesar's house.
14 ANTONY: And thither will I straight to visit him.
15   He comes upon a wish. Fortune is merry,
16   And in this mood will give us anything.
17 SERVANT: I heard him say Brutus and Cassius
18   Are rid like madmen through the gates of Rome.
19 ANTONY: Belike they had some notice of the people,
20   How I had mov'd them. Bring me to Octavius. *(Exit
21   ANTONY and SERVANT)*
22
23
24
25
26
27
28
29
30
31
32
33
34
35

Othello
Act III, Scene 3

CHARACTERS

Desdemona — daughter of Senator Brabantio of Venice and the wife of General Othello. Desdemona is considered by some to be innocent and naive; others say she is blinded by her deep love for her husband Othello, who is a Moor — a man of another race or color.

Emilia — wife of the villainous Iago. She is outspoken, somewhat annoying, and oftentimes cynical, probably due to the years of living with her husband. She is also Desdemona's friend and confidante.

Cassio — a young and handsome lieutenant in Othello's army.

Othello — a general in the Venetian army. He is a seasoned warrior, an honest man, and is newly married to Desdemona.

Iago — He is considered by many to be Shakespeare's consummate villain. He is conniving, two-faced, and cannot be trusted. Also, he is married to Emilia.

This scene, oftentimes referred to as the "temptation scene," is one of the most famous in all of drama. It shows how a man, despite his power in the military and the respect he receives from society, can be deceived into believing that his wife had been unfaithful. Othello is indeed considered wise because of his rise in the military ranks; however, Iago, the conniving villain, sees that his wisdom is clouded by his deep love for his new bride, Desdemona.

Iago is upset: he has been overlooked for promotion in Othello's army; to make matters worse, Cassio, who Iago believes is a lesser soldier, has been appointed to lieutenant by Othello. Because of this, he vows revenge and designs a plot to hurt both Cassio and Othello.

This scene opens in the castle garden, and Desdemona is promising Cassio that she can persuade Othello to reinstate him to rank of lieutenant. (He lost the rank after accidentally wounding Montano, the governor of Cyprus, in a drunken brawl while trying to seem a good soldier and friend to Iago.) As Othello and Iago enter, Cassio leaves hurriedly. After Cassio exits, Desdemona begins her plea to Othello for Cassio's reinstatement.

However, after Desdemona and Emilia leave, Iago begins his sinister plot. He begins dropping hints and innuendos that Desdemona is possibly having an affair with Cassio, and, in many ways, he begins to undermine Othello's faith in Desdemona's innocence.

Iago exits and Desdemona returns. Othello complains of having a headache, and she tries to soothe it by placing her cherished straw-berry-embroidered handkerchief (one given to her by Othello) to his head. Othello angrily pushes it away from his head and it falls, unnoticed, to the floor. As they depart, it is left behind. (This is very important!)

Emilia enters, notices the handkerchief, and innocently gives it to her husband Iago. After she exits, Othello reenters and demands Iago to give proof of Desdemona's infidelity. Iago responds to this by claim-ing that he overheard Cassio talking in his sleep about making love to Desdemona. He also says that he has seen Cassio wipe his beard with a strawberry-embroidered handkerchief. Enraged, Othello falls to his knees. He is joined by Iago, and together they vow revenge: furthermore, Othello promises that Iago will be his new lieutenant.

When performing this scene, it is important to note how clever and conniving Iago really is: he seizes the opportunity of Desdemona innocently speaking of Cassio and plants the seed of distrust in Othello. He knows that man, being human, is flawed and subject to fears and irrational suspicions.

1   ***SETTING:***   Cyprus. The garden of the Castle.
2   ***AT RISE:***   Enter Desdemona, Cassio, and Emilia.
3
4   DESDEMONA: Be thou assured, good Cassio, I will do
5   All my abilities in thy behalf.
6   EMILIA: Good madam, do. I warrant it grieves my husband
7   As if the cause were his.
8   DESDEMONA: O, that's an honest fellow. Do not doubt,
9   Cassio,
10   But I will have my lord and you again
11   As friendly as you were.
12   CASSIO: Bounteous madam,
13   Whatever shall become of Michael Cassio,
14   He's never anything but your true servant.
15   DESDEMONA: I know't; I thank you. You do love my lord;
16   You have known him long; and be you well assured
17   He shall in strangeness stand no farther off
18   Than in politic distance.
19   CASSIO: Ay, but, lady,
20   That policy may either last so long,
21   Or feed upon such nice and waterish diet,
22   Or breed itself so out of circumstance,
23   That, I being absent, and my place supplied,
24   My general will forget my love and service.
25   DESDEMONA: Do not doubt that. Before Emilia here
26   I give thee warrant of thy place. Assure thee,
27   If I do vow a friendship, I'll perform it
28   To the last article. My lord shall never rest;
29   I'll watch him tame and talk him out of patience;
30   His bed shall seem a school, his board a shrift;
31   I'll intermingle everything he does
32   With Cassio's suit. Therefore be merry, Cassio,
33   For thy solicitor shall rather die
34   Than give thy cause away. *(Enter OTHELLO and IAGO)*
35   EMILIA: Madam, here comes my lord.

1 CASSIO: Madam, I'll take my leave.

2 DESDEMONA: Why, stay, and hear me speak.

3 CASSIO: Madam, not now. I am very ill at ease,

4   Unfit for mine own purposes.

5 DESDEMONA: Well, do your discretion. *(Exit CASSIO)*

6 IAGO: Ha! I like not that.

7 OTHELLO: What dost thou say?

8 IAGO: Nothing, my lord; or if — I know not what.

9 OTHELLO: Was not that Cassio parted from my wife?

10 IAGO: Cassio, my lord? No, sure, I cannot think it,

11   That he would steal away so guilty-like,

12   Seeing you coming.

13 OTHELLO: I do believe 'twas he.

14 DESDEMONA: How now, my lord?

15   I have been talking with a suitor here,

16   A man that languishes in your displeasure.

17 OTHELLO: Who is't you mean?

18 DESDEMONA: Why, your lieutenant, Cassio. Good my lord,

19   If I have any grace or power to move you,

20   His present reconciliation take;

21   For if he be not one that truly loves you,

22   That errs in ignorance, and not in cunning,

23   I have no judgment in an honest face.

24   I prithee call him back.

25 OTHELLO: Went he hence now?

26 DESDEMONA: Yes, faith; so humbled

27   That he hath left part of his grief with me

28   To suffer with him. Good love, call him back.

29 OTHELLO: Not now, sweet Desdemon; some other time.

30 DESDEMONA: But shall't be shortly?

31 OTHELLO: The sooner, sweet, for you.

32 DESDEMONA: Shall't be tonight at supper?

33 OTHELLO: No, not tonight.

34 DESDEMONA: Tomorrow dinner then?

35 OTHELLO: I shall not dine at home.

1   I meet the captains at the citadel.

2 DESDEMONA: Why then, tomorrow night, or Tuesday morn,

3   Or Tuesday noon or night, or Wednesday morn.

4   I prithee name the time, but let it not

5   Exceed three days. I' faith, he's penitent;

6   And yet his trespass, in our common reason

7   (Save that, they say, the wars must make examples

8   Out of their best) is not almost a fault

9   T' incur a private check. When shall he come?

10   Tell me, Othello. I wonder in my soul

11   What you could ask me that I should deny

12   Or stand so mamm'ring on. What? Michael Cassio,

13   That came a-wooing with you, and so many a time,

14   When I have spoke of you dispraisingly,

15   Hath ta'en your part — to have so much to do

16   To bring him in? Trust me, I could do much —

17 OTHELLO: Prithee no more. Let him come when he will!

18   I will deny thee nothing.

19 DESDEMONA: Why, this is not a boon;

20   'Tis as I should entreat you wear your gloves,

21   Or feed on nourishing dishes, or keep you warm,

22   Or sue to you to do a peculiar profit

23   To your own person. Nay, when I have a suit

24   Wherein I mean to touch your love indeed,

25   It shall be full of poise and difficult weight,

26   And fearful to be granted.

27 OTHELLO: I will deny thee nothing!

28   Whereon I do beseech thee grant me this,

29   To leave me but a little to myself.

30 DESDEMONA: Shall I deny you? No. Farewell, my lord.

31 OTHELLO: Farewell, my Desdemon. I'll come to thee straight.

32 DESDEMONA: Emilia, come. — Be as your fancies teach you.

33   Whate'er you be, I am obedient. *(Exit DESDEMONA and*

34   *EMILIA)*

35 OTHELLO: Excellent wretch! Perdition catch my soul

1	But I do love thee! and when I love thee not,
2	Chaos is come again.
3	IAGO: My noble lord —
4	OTHELLO: What dost thou say, Iago?
5	IAGO: Did Michael Cassio, when you wooed my lady,
6	Know of your love?
7	OTHELLO: He did, from first to last. Why dost thou ask?
8	IAGO: But for a satisfaction of my thought;
9	No further harm.
10	OTHELLO: Why of thy thought, Iago?
11	IAGO: I did not think he had been acquainted with her.
12	OTHELLO: O, yes, and went between us very oft.
13	IAGO: Indeed?
14	OTHELLO: Indeed? Ay, indeed! Discern'st thou aught in that?
15	Is he not honest?
16	IAGO: Honest, my lord?
17	OTHELLO: Honest? Ay, honest.
18	IAGO: My lord, for aught I know.
19	OTHELLO: What dost thou think?
20	IAGO: Think, my lord?
21	OTHELLO: Think, my lord?
22	By heaven, he echoes me,
23	As if there were some monster in his thought
24	Too hideous to be shown. Thou dost mean something.
25	I heard thee say even now, thou lik'st not that,
26	When Cassio left my wife. What didst not like?
27	And when I told thee he was of my counsel
28	In my whole course of wooing, thou cried'st "Indeed?"
29	And didst contract and purse thy brow together,
30	As if thou then hadst shut up in thy brain
31	Some horrible conceit. If thou dost love me,
32	Show me thy thought.
33	IAGO: My lord, you know I love you.
34	OTHELLO: I think thou dost;
35	And, for I know thou'rt full of love and honesty

1	And weigh'st thy words before thou giv'st them breath,
2	Therefore these stops of thine fright me the more;
3	For such things in a false disloyal knave
4	Are tricks of custom; but in a man that's just
5	They are close dilations, working from the heart
6	That passion cannot rule.
7	IAGO: For Michael Cassio,
8	I dare be sworn I think that he is honest.
9	OTHELLO: I think so too.
10	IAGO: Men should be what they seem;
11	Or those that be not, would they might seem none!
12	OTHELLO: Certain, men should be what they seem.
13	IAGO: Why then, I think Cassio's an honest man.
14	OTHELLO: Nay, yet there's more in this.
15	I prithee speak to me, as to thy thinkings,
16	As thou dost ruminate, and give thy worst of thoughts
17	The worst of words.
18	IAGO: Good my lord, pardon me.
19	Though I am bound to every act of duty,
20	I am not bound to that all slaves are free to.
21	Utter my thoughts? Why, say they are vile and false,
22	As where's that palace whereinto foul things
23	Sometimes intrude not? Who has a breast so pure
24	But some uncleanly apprehensions
25	Keep leets and law days, and in session sit
26	With meditations lawful?
27	OTHELLO: Thou dost conspire against thy friend, Iago,
28	If thou but think'st him wronged, and mak'st his ear
29	A stranger to thy thoughts.
30	IAGO: I do beseech you —
31	Though I perchance am vicious in my guess
32	(As I confess it is my nature's plague
33	To spy into abuses, and oft my jealousy
34	Shapes faults that are not) — that your wisdom
35	From one that so imperfectly conceits

1	Would take no notice, nor build yourself a trouble
2	Out of his scattering and unsure observance.
3	It were not for your quiet nor your good,
4	Nor for my manhood, honesty, or wisdom,
5	To let you know my thoughts.
6	OTHELLO: What dost thou mean?
7	IAGO: Good name in man and woman, dear my lord,
8	Is the immediate jewel of their souls.
9	Who steals my purse steals trash; 'tis something, nothing;
10	'Twas mine, 'tis his, and has been slave to thousands;
11	But he that filches from me my good name
12	Robs me of that which not enriches him
13	And makes me poor indeed.
14	OTHELLO: By heaven, I'll know thy thoughts!
15	IAGO: You cannot, if my heart were in your hand;
16	Nor shall not whilst 'tis in my custody.
17	OTHELLO: Ha!
18	IAGO: O, beware, my lord, of jealousy!
19	It is the green-eyed monster, which doth mock
20	The meat it feeds on. That cuckold lives in bliss
21	Who, certain of his fate, loves not his wronger;
22	But O, what damned minutes tells he o'er
23	Who dotes, yet doubts; suspects, yet strongly loves!
24	OTHELLO: O misery!
25	IAGO: Poor and content is rich, and rich enough;
26	But riches fineless is as poor as winter
27	To him that ever fears he shall be poor.
28	Good heaven, the souls of all my tribe defend
29	From jealousy!
30	OTHELLO: Why, why is this?
31	Think'st thou I'd make a life of jealousy,
32	To follow still the changes of the moon
33	With fresh suspicions? No! To be once in doubt
34	Is once to be resolved. Exchange me for a goat
35	When I shall turn the business of my soul

1   To such exsufflicate and blown surmises,

2   Matching thy inference. 'Tis not to make me jealous

3   To say my wife is fair, feeds well, loves company,

4   Is free of speech, sings, plays, and dances well.

5   Where virtue is, these are more virtuous.

6   Nor from mine own weak merits will I draw

7   The smallest fear or doubt of her revolt,

8   For she had eyes, and chose me. No, Iago;

9   I'll see before I doubt; when I doubt, prove;

10   And on the proof there is no more but this —

11   Away at once with love or jealousy!

12 IAGO: I am glad of it; for now I shall have reason

13   To show the love and duty that I bear you

14   With franker spirit. Therefore, as I am bound,

15   Receive it from me. I speak not yet of proof.

16   Look to your wife; observe her well with Cassio;

17   Wear your eye thus, not jealous nor secure.

18   I would not have your free and noble nature,

19   Out of self-bounty, be abused. Look to't.

20   I know our country disposition well:

21   In Venice they do let heaven see the pranks

22   They dare not show their husbands; their best conscience

23   Is not to leave't undone, but keep't unknown.

24 OTHELLO: Dost thou say so?

25 IAGO: She did deceive her father, marrying you;

26   And when she seemed to shake and fear your looks,

27   She loved them most.

28 OTHELLO: And so she did.

29 IAGO: Why, go to then!

30   She that, so young, could give out such a seeming

31   To seel her father's eyes up close as oak —

32   He thought 'twas witchcraft — but I am much to blame.

33   I humbly do beseech you of your pardon

34   For too much loving you.

35 OTHELLO: I am bound to thee for ever.

1	IAGO: I see this hath a little dashed your spirits.
2	OTHELLO: Not a jot, not a jot.
3	IAGO: I' faith, I fear it has.
4	I hope you will consider what is spoke
5	Comes from my love. But I do see y'are moved.
6	I am to pray you not to strain my speech
7	To grosser issues nor to larger reach
8	Than to suspicion.
9	OTHELLO: I will not.
10	IAGO: Should you do so, my lord,
11	My speech should fall into such vile success
12	As my thoughts aim not at. Cassio's my worthy friend —
13	My lord, I see y'are moved.
14	OTHELLO: No, not much moved.
15	I do not think but Desdemona's honest.
16	IAGO: Long live she so! and long live you to think so!
17	OTHELLO: And yet, how nature erring from itself —
18	IAGO: Ay, there's the point! as (to be bold with you)
19	Not to affect many proposed matches
20	Of her own clime, complexion, and degree,
21	Whereto we see in all things nature tends —
22	Foh! one may smell in such a will most rank,
23	Foul disproportion, thoughts unnatural —
24	But pardon me — I do not in position
25	Distinctly speak of her; though I may fear
26	Her will, recoiling to her better judgment,
27	May fall to match you with her country forms,
28	And happily repent.
29	OTHELLO: Farewell, farewell!
30	If more thou dost perceive, let me know more.
31	Set on thy wife to observe. Leave me, Iago.
32	IAGO: My lord, I take my leave. *(IAGO walks away.)*
33	OTHELLO: Why did I marry? This honest creature doubtless
34	Sees and knows more, much more, than he unfolds.
35	IAGO: *(Returns.)* My lord, I would I might entreat your Honor

1	To scan this thing no further. Leave it to time.
2	Although 'tis fit that Cassio have his place,
3	For sure he fills it up with great ability,
4	Yet, if you please to hold him off awhile,
5	You shall by that perceive him and his means.
6	Note if your lady strain his entertainment
7	With any strong or vehement importunity.
8	Much will be seen in that. In the mean time
9	Let me be thought too busy in my fears
10	(As worthy cause I have to fear I am)
11	And hold her free, I do beseech your Honor.
12	OTHELLO: Fear not my government.
13	IAGO: I once more take my leave. *(He exits.)*
14	OTHELLO: This fellow's of exceeding honesty,
15	And knows all qualities, with a learned spirit
16	Of human dealings. If I do prove her haggard,
17	Though that her jesses were my dear heartstrings,
18	I'd whistle her off and let her down the wind
19	To prey at fortune. Haply, for I am black
20	And have not those soft parts of conversation
21	That chamberers have, or for I am declined
22	Into the vale of years (yet that's not much),
23	She's gone. I am abused, and my relief
24	Must be to loathe her. O curse of marriage,
25	That we can call these delicate creatures ours,
26	And not their appetites! I had rather be a toad
27	And live upon the vapor of a dungeon
28	Than keep a corner in the thing I love
29	For others' uses. Yet 'tis the plague of great ones;
30	Prerogatived are they less than the base.
31	'Tis destiny unshunnable, like death:
32	Even then this forked plague is fated to us
33	When we do quicken. Desdemona comes. *(Enter DES-*
34	*DEMONA and EMILIA)*
35	If she be false, O, then heaven mocks itself!

1   I'll not believe't.

2 DESDEMONA: How now, my dear Othello?

3   Your dinner, and the generous islanders

4   By you invited, do attend your presence.

5 OTHELLO: I am to blame.

6 DESDEMONA: Why do you speak so faintly?

7   Are you not well?

8 OTHELLO: I have a pain upon my forehead, here.

9 DESDEMONA: Faith, that's with watching; 'twill away again.

10   Let me but bind it hard, within this hour

11   It will be well.

12 OTHELLO: Your napkin is too little. *(He pushes it away and it*

13   *drops.)*

14   Let it alone. Come, I'll go in with you.

15 DESDEMONA: I am very sorry that you are not well. *(Exit*

16   *OTHELLO and DESDEMONA)*

17 EMILIA: I am glad I have found this napkin.

18   This was her first remembrance from the Moor.

19   My wayward husband hath a hundred times

20   Wooed me to steal it; but she so loves the token

21   (For he conjured her she should ever keep it)

22   That she reserves it evermore about her

23   To kiss and talk to. I'll have the work ta'en out

24   And give't Iago.

25   What he will do with it heaven knows, not I;

26   I nothing but to please his fantasy. *(Enter IAGO)*

27 IAGO: How now? What do you here alone?

28 EMILIA: Do not you chide; I have a thing for you.

29 IAGO: A thing for me? It is a common thing —

30 EMILIA: Ha?

31 IAGO: To have a foolish wife.

32 EMILIA: O, is that all? What will you give me now

33   For that same handkerchief?

34 IAGO: What handkerchief?

35 EMILIA: What handkerchief?

1   Why, that the Moor first gave to Desdemona;
2   That which so often you did bid me steal.
3 IAGO: Hast stol'n it from her?
4 EMILIA: No, faith; she let it drop by negligence,
5   And to th' advantage, I, being here, took't up.
6   Look, here it is.
7 IAGO: A good wench! Give it me.
8 EMILIA: What will you do with't, that you have been so
9   earnest
10   To have me filch it?
11 IAGO: Why, what's that to you? *(Snatches it.)*
12 EMILIA: If it be not for some purpose of import,
13   Give't me again. Poor lady, she'll run mad
14   When she shall lack it.
15 IAGO: Be not you acknown on't; I have use for it.
16   Go, leave me. *(Exit EMILIA)*
17   I will in Cassio's lodging lose this napkin
18   And let him find it. Trifles light as air
19   Are to the jealous confirmations strong
20   As proofs of holy writ. This may do something.
21   The Moor already changes with my poison.
22   Dangerous conceits are in their natures poisons
23   Which at the first are scarce found to distaste,
24   But with a little act upon the blood
25   Burn like the mines of sulphur. *(Enter OTHELLO)* I did
26   say so.
27   Look where he comes! Not poppy nor mandragora,
28   Nor all the drowsy syrups of the world,
29   Shall ever medicine thee to that sweet sleep
30   Which thou ow'dst yesterday.
31 OTHELLO: Ha! ha! false to me?
32 IAGO: Why, how now, General? No more of that!
33 OTHELLO: Avaunt! be gone! Thou hast set me on the rack.
34   I swear 'tis better to be much abused
35   Than but to know't a little.

1   IAGO: How now, my lord?
2   OTHELLO: What sense had I of her stol'n hours of lust?
3   I saw't not, thought it not, it harmed not me.
4   I slept the next night well, was free and merry;
5   I found not Cassio's kisses on her lips.
6   He that is robbed, not wanting what is stol'n,
7   Let him not know't, and he's not robbed at all.
8   IAGO: I am sorry to hear this.
9   OTHELLO: I had been happy if the general camp,
10   Pioners and all, had tasted her sweet body,
11   So I had nothing known. O, now for ever
12   Farewell the tranquil mind! farewell content!
13   Farewell the plumed troop, and the big wars
14   That make ambition virtue! O, farewell!
15   Farewell the neighing steed and the shrill trump,
16   The spirit-stirring drum, th' ear-piercing fife,
17   The royal banner, and all quality,
18   Pride, pomp, and circumstance of glorious war!
19   And O ye mortal engines whose rude throats
20   Th' immortal Jove's dread clamors counterfeit,
21   Farewell! Othello's occupation's gone!
22   IAGO: Is't possible, my lord?
23   OTHELLO: Villain, be sure thou prove my love a whore!
24   Be sure of it; give me the ocular proof;
25   Or, by the worth of man's eternal soul,
26   Thou hadst been better have been born a dog
27   Than answer my waked wrath!
28   IAGO: Is't come to this?
29   OTHELLO: Make me to see't; or at the least so prove it
30   That the probation bear no hinge nor loop
31   To hang a doubt on — or woe upon thy life!
32   IAGO: My noble lord —
33   OTHELLO: If thou dost slander her and torture me,
34   Never pray more; abandon all remorse;
35   On horror's head horrors accumulate;

1 Do deeds to make heaven weep, all earth amazed;
2 For nothing canst thou to damnation add
3 Greater than that.
4 IAGO: O grace! O heaven forgive me!
5 Are you a man? Have you a soul or sense? —
6 God b' wi' you! take mine office. O wretched fool,
7 That liv'st to make thine honesty a vice!
8 O monstrous world! Take note, take note, O world,
9 To be direct and honest is not safe.
10 I thank you for this profit; and from hence
11 I'll love no friend, sith love breeds such offense.
12 OTHELLO: Nay, stay. Thou shouldst be honest.
13 IAGO: I should be wise; for honesty's a fool
14 And loses that it works for.
15 OTHELLO: By the world,
16 I think my wife be honest, and think she is not;
17 I think that thou art just, and think thou art not.
18 I'll have some proof. Her name, that was as fresh
19 As Dian's visage, is now begrimed and black
20 As mine own face. If there be cords, or knives,
21 Poison, or fire, or suffocating streams,
22 I'll not endure it. Would I were satisfied!
23 IAGO: I see, sir, you are eaten up with passion.
24 I do repent me that I put it to you.
25 You would be satisfied?
26 OTHELLO: Would? Nay, I will.
27 IAGO: And may. But how? how satisfied, my lord?
28 Would you, the supervisor, grossly gape on?
29 Behold her topped?
30 OTHELLO: Death and damnation! O!
31 IAGO: It were a tedious difficulty, I think,
32 To bring them to that prospect. Damn them then,
33 If ever mortal eyes do see them bolster
34 More than their own! What then? How then?
35 What shall I say? Where's satisfaction?

1	It is impossible you should see this,
2	Were they as prime as goats, as hot as monkeys,
3	As salt as wolves in pride, and fools as gross
4	As ignorance made drunk. But yet, I say,
5	If imputation and strong circumstances
6	Which lead directly to the door of truth
7	Will give you satisfaction, you may have't.
8	OTHELLO: Give me a living reason she's disloyal.
9	IAGO: I do not like the office.
10	But sith I am entered in this cause so far,
11	Pricked to't by foolish honesty and love,
12	I will go on. I lay with Cassio lately,
13	And being troubled with a raging tooth,
14	I could not sleep.
15	There are a kind of men so loose of soul
16	That in their sleeps will mutter their affairs.
17	One of this kind is Cassio.
18	In sleep I heard him say, "Sweet Desdemona,
19	Let us be wary, let us hide our loves!"
20	And then, sir, would he gripe and wring my hand,
21	Cry "O sweet creature!" and then kiss me hard,
22	As if he plucked up kisses by the roots
23	That grew upon my lips; then laid his leg
24	Over my thigh, and sighed, and kissed, and then
25	Cried "Cursed fate that gave thee to the Moor!"
26	OTHELLO: O monstrous! monstrous!
27	IAGO: Nay, this was but his dream.
28	OTHELLO: But this denoted a foregone conclusion.
29	'Tis a shrewd doubt, though it be but a dream.
30	IAGO: And this may help to thicken other proofs
31	That do demonstrate thinly.
32	OTHELLO: I'll tear her all to pieces!
33	IAGO: Nay, but be wise. Yet we see nothing done;
34	She may be honest yet. Tell me but this —
35	Have you not sometimes seen a handkerchief

1   Spotted with strawberries in your wive's hand?

2 OTHELLO: I gave her such a one; 'twas my first gift.

3 IAGO: I know not that; but such a handkerchief

4   (I am sure it was your wive's) did I today

5   See Cassio wipe his beard with.

6 OTHELLO: If't be that —

7 IAGO: If it be that, or any that was hers,

8   It speaks against her, with the other proofs.

9 OTHELLO: O, that the slave had forty thousand lives!

10   One is too poor, too weak for my revenge.

11   Now do I see 'tis true. Look here, Iago:

12   All my fond love thus do I blow to heaven.

13   'Tis gone.

14   Arise, black vengeance, from the hollow hell!

15   Yield up, O love, thy crown and hearted throne

16   To tyrannous hate! Swell, bosom, with thy fraught,

17   For 'tis of aspics' tongues!

18 IAGO: Yet be content.

19 OTHELLO: O, blood, blood, blood!

20 IAGO: Patience, I say. Your mind perhaps may change.

21 OTHELLO: Never, Iago. Like to the Pontic sea,

22   Whose icy current and compulsive course

23   Ne'er feels retiring ebb, but keeps due on

24   To the Propontic and the Hellespont;

25   Even so my bloody thoughts, with violent pace,

26   Shall ne'er look back, ne'er ebb to humble love,

27   Till that a capable and wide revenge

28   Swallow them up. *(He kneels.)* Now, by yond marble heaven,

29   In the due reverence of a sacred vow

30   I here engage my words.

31 IAGO: Do not rise yet. *(IAGO kneels.)*

32   Witness, you ever-burning lights above,

33   You elements that clip us round about,

34   Witness that here Iago doth give up

35   The execution of his wit, hands, heart

1   **To wronged Othello's service! Let him command,**

2   **And to obey shall be in me remorse,**

3   **What bloody business ever.** *(They rise.)*

4 **OTHELLO:**   **I greet thy love,**

5   **Not with vain thanks but with acceptance bounteous,**

6   **And will upon the instant put thee to't.**

7   **Within these three days let me hear thee say**

8   **That Cassio's not alive.**

9 **IAGO:**   **My friend is dead; 'tis done at your request.**

10   **But let her live.**

11 **OTHELLO:**   **Damn her, lewd minx! O, damn her!**

12   **Come, go with me apart. I will withdraw**

13   **To furnish me with some swift means of death**

14   **For the fair devil. Now art thou my lieutenant.**

15 **IAGO:**   **I am your own for ever.** *(They exit.)*

16

17

18

19

20

21

22

23

24

25

26

27

28

29

30

31

32

33

34

35

Othello
Act III, Scene 4

MAJOR CHARACTERS

Desdemona — daughter of Senator Brabantio of Venice and the wife of general Othello. Desdemona is considered by some to be innocent and naive; others say she is blinded by her deep love for her husband Othello, who is a Moor — a man of another race or color.

Emilia — wife of the villainous Iago. She is outspoken, somewhat annoying, and oftentimes cynical, probably due to the years of living with her husband. She is also Desdemona's friend and confidante.

Cassio — a young and handsome lieutenant in Othello's army

Othello — a general in the Venetian army. He is a seasoned warrior, an honest man, and is newly married to Desdemona.

Iago — He is considered by many to be Shakespeare's consummate villain. He is conniving, two-faced, and cannot be trusted. Also, he is married to Emilia.

MINOR CHARACTERS

Bianca — Cassio's current mistress

Clown — a punster. He fetches Cassio.

In order to fully understand this scene, and more importantly, the implications of the "lost handkerchief," one must know what has previously transpired.

Iago is bent on a mission: to destroy Cassio and, ultimately, Othello. Iago is a soldier in the Army of Venice of which Othello is general. He is furious that Cassio, a fellow soldier and friend, was promoted to lieutenant before him.

In order to see Iago's plan of revenge, one must first of all understand how conniving and mistrusting he is. (As a matter of fact, many literary critics consider Iago to be Shakespeare's most villainous character.) Iago has witnessed Othello's new wife innocently speaking of Cassio; to be sure, Desdemona is trying to have Cassio forgiven by Othello for accidentally wounding the governor of Cyprus, and, with his forgiveness, to be reinstated to the rank of lieutenant. However, Iago seizes the opportunity to plant a seed of jealousy in Othello — he tells Othello that he believes that Cassio and Desdemona are having an affair. He says that he heard Cassio talking in his sleep about making love to Desdemona; he also says that he has seen Cassio wipe his beard with a strawberry-embroidered handkerchief. (The handkerchief plays an important role in this play: it was a gift from Othello to Desdemona, and she cherishes it dearly. However, in the previous scene, it ended up in Iago's possession and he plans to plant it in Cassio's room.)

In this scene, Desdemona again talks to Othello about reinstating Cassio; however, Othello's mood is dark and brooding — he is angry that Desdemona cannot produce the handkerchief at his request. He then tells her that the handkerchief used to belong to his mother and it contains great magical powers that could harm the owner if the handkerchief were to be lost. This alarms the innocent and naive Desdemona; remember that she is newly married to Othello and is charmed by his dark, Moorish looks.

As Othello continues to ask Desdemona for the handkerchief, his anger grows more intense and furious. Emilia, Iago's wife, is with Desdemona and witnesses Othello's fury, but dismisses it as being typical of any man. (It is important to note that Desdemona has no idea that Othello suspects her of having an affair with Cassio; she thinks he is simply angry about losing the handkerchief and is confused by his sudden outburst.)

When the ladies have gone, Cassio meets Bianca, his current mistress, who scolds him for neglecting her for a week. Cassio changes the subject and gives her a handkerchief that he found in his room, asking her to make a copy of the embroidery. Bianca is disturbed at his neglecting her, but she nevertheless agrees to do what he asks.

1 **SETTING:** Cyprus. Before the castle.
2 **AT RISE:** Enter Desdemona, Emilia, and Clown.
3
4 DESDEMONA: Do you know, sirrah, where Lieutenant
5   Cassio lies?
6 CLOWN: I dare not say he lies anywhere.
7 DESDEMONA: Why man?
8 CLOWN: He's a soldier; and for one to say a soldier lies is
9   stabbing.
10 DESDEMONA: Go to. Where lodges he?
11 CLOWN: To tell you where he lodges is to tell you where I lie.
12 DESDEMONA: Can anything be made of this?
13 CLOWN: I know not where he lodges; and for me to devise a
14   lodging, and say he lies here or he lies there, were to lie
15   in mine own throat.
16 DESDEMONA: Can you enquire him out, and be edified by
17   report?
18 CLOWN: I will catechize the world for him; that is, make
19   questions, and by them answer.
20 DESDEMONA: Seek him, bid him come hither. Tell him I have
21   moved my lord on his behalf and hope all will be well.
22 CLOWN: To do this is within the compass of man's wit, and
23   therefore I'll attempt the doing it. *(He exits.)*
24 DESDEMONA: Where should I lose that handkerchief,
25   Emilia?
26 EMILIA: I know not, madam.
27 DESDEMONA: Believe me, I had rather have lost my purse
28   Full of crusadoes; and but my noble Moor
29   Is true of mind, and made of no such baseness
30   As jealous creatures are, it were enough
31   To put him to ill thinking.
32 EMILIA: Is he not jealous?
33 DESDEMONA: Who? he? I think the sun where he was born
34   Drew all such humors from him. *(Enter OTHELLO)*
35 EMILIA: Look where he comes.

1   DESDEMONA: I will not leave him now till Cassio
2   Be called to him. — How is't with you, my lord?
3   OTHELLO: Well, my good lady. *(Aside)* O, hardness to
4   dissemble! —
5   How do you, Desdemona?
6   DESDEMONA: Well, my good lord.
7   OTHELLO: Give me your hand. This hand is moist, my lady.
8   DESDEMONA: It yet hath felt no age nor known no sorrow.
9   OTHELLO: This argues fruitfulness and liberal heart.
10   Hot, hot, and moist. This hand of yours requires
11   A sequester from liberty, fasting and prayer,
12   Much castigation, exercise devout;
13   For here's a young and sweating devil here
14   That commonly rebels. 'Tis a good hand,
15   A frank one.
16   DESDEMONA: You may, indeed, say so;
17   For 'twas that hand that gave away my heart.
18   OTHELLO: A liberal hand! The hearts of old gave hands;
19   But our new heraldry is hands, not hearts.
20   DESDEMONA: I cannot speak of this. Come now, your
21   promise!
22   OTHELLO: What promise, chuck?
23   DESDEMONA: I have sent to bid Cassio come speak with you.
24   OTHELLO: I have a salt and sorry rheum offends me.
25   Lend me thy handkerchief.
26   DESDEMONA: Here, my lord.
27   OTHELLO: That which I gave you.
28   DESDEMONA: I have it not about me.
29   OTHELLO: Not?
30   DESDEMONA: No indeed, my lord.
31   OTHELLO: That is a fault.
32   That handkerchief
33   Did an Egyptian to my mother give.
34   She was a charmer, and could almost read
35   The thoughts of people. She told her, while she kept it,

1	'Twould make her amiable and subdue my father
2	Entirely to her love; but if she lost it
3	Or made a gift of it, my father's eye
4	Should hold her loathed, and his spirits should hunt
5	After new fancies. She, dying, gave it me,
6	And bid me, when my fate would have me wive,
7	To give it her. I did so; and take heed on't;
8	Make it a darling like your precious eye.
9	To lose't or give't away were such perdition
10	As nothing else could match.
11	DESDEMONA: Is't possible?
12	OTHELLO: 'Tis true. There's magic in the web of it.
13	A sibyl that had numb'red in the world
14	The sun to course two hundred compasses,
15	In her prophetic fury sewed the work;
16	The worms were hallowed that did breed the silk;
17	And it was dyed in mummy which the skilful
18	Conserved of maidens' hearts.
19	DESDEMONA: I' faith? Is't true?
20	OTHELLO: Most veritable. Therefore look to't well.
21	DESDEMONA: Then would to God that I had never seen't!
22	OTHELLO: Ha! Wherefore?
23	DESDEMONA: Why do you speak so startingly and rash?
24	OTHELLO: Is't lost? Is't gone? Speak, is it out o' th' way?
25	DESDEMONA: Heaven bless us!
26	OTHELLO: Say you?
27	DESDEMONA: It is not lost. But what an if it were?
28	OTHELLO: How?
29	DESDEMONA: I say it is not lost.
30	OTHELLO: Fetch't, let me see't!
31	DESDEMONA: Why, so I can, sir; but I will not now.
32	This is a trick to put me from my suit.
33	Pray you let Cassio be received again.
34	OTHELLO: Fetch me the handkerchief! My mind misgives.
35	DESDEMONA: Come, come!

1   You'll never meet a more sufficient man.

2   OTHELLO: The handkerchief!

3   DESDEMONA: I pray talk me of Cassio.

4   OTHELLO: The handkerchief!

5   DESDEMONA: A man that all his time

6   Hath founded his good fortunes on your love,

7   Shared dangers with you —

8   OTHELLO: The handkerchief!

9   DESDEMONA: In sooth, you are to blame.

10   OTHELLO: Away! *(He exits.)*

11   EMILIA: Is not this man jealous?

12   DESDEMONA: I ne'er saw this before.

13   Sure there's some wonder in this handkerchief.

14   I am most unhappy in the loss of it.

15   EMILIA: 'Tis not a year or two shows us a man.

16   They are all but stomachs, and we all but food;

17   They eat us hungerly, and when they are full,

18   They belch us. *(Enter IAGO and CASSIO)* Look you —

19   Cassio and my husband!

20   IAGO: There is no other way; 'tis she must do't.

21   And lo the happiness! Go and importune her.

22   DESDEMONA: How now, good Cassio? What's the news with

23   you?

24   CASSIO: Madam, my former suit. I do beseech you

25   That by your virtuous means I may again

26   Exist, and be a member of his love

27   Whom I with all the office of my heart

28   Entirely honor. I would not be delayed.

29   If my offense be of such mortal kind

30   That neither service past, nor present sorrows,

31   Nor purposed merit in futurity,

32   Can ransom me into his love again,

33   But to know so must be my benefit.

34   So shall I clothe me in a forced content,

35   And shut myself up in some other course,

1	To fortune's alms.
2	DESDEMONA: Alas, thrice-gentle Cassio!
3	My advocation is not now in tune.
4	My lord is not my lord; nor should I know him,
5	Were he in favor as in humor altered.
6	So help me every spirit sanctified
7	As I have spoken for you all my best
8	And stood within the blank of his displeasure
9	For my free speech! You must awhile be patient.
10	What I can do I will; and more I will
11	Than for myself I dare. Let that suffice you.
12	IAGO: Is my lord angry?
13	EMILIA: He went hence but now,
14	And certainly in strange unquietness.
15	IAGO: Can he be angry? I have seen the cannon
16	When it hath blown his ranks into the air
17	And, like the devil, from his very arm
18	Puffed his own brother — and can he be angry?
19	Something of moment then. I will go meet him.
20	There's matter in't indeed if he be angry.
21	DESDEMONA: I prithee do so. *(Exit IAGO)* Something sure of
22	state,
23	Either from Venice or some unhatched practice
24	Made demonstrable here in Cyprus to him,
25	Hath puddled his clear spirit; and in such cases
26	Men's natures wrangle with inferior things,
27	Though great ones are their object. 'Tis even so.
28	For let our finger ache, and it endues
29	Our other healthful members even to that sense
30	Of pain. Nay, we must think men are not gods,
31	Nor of them look for such observancy
32	As fits the bridal. Beshrew me much, Emilia,
33	I was (unhandsome warrior as I am!)
34	Arraigning his unkindness with my soul;
35	But now I find I had suborned the witness,

1   And he's indicted falsely.
2   EMILIA: Pray heaven it be state matters, as you think,
3   And no conception nor no jealous toy
4   Concerning you.
5   DESDEMONA: Alas the day! I never gave him cause.
6   EMILIA: But jealous souls will not be answered so.
7   They are not ever jealous for the cause,
8   But jealous for they are jealous. 'Tis a monster
9   Begot upon itself, born on itself.
10   DESDEMONA: Heaven keep that monster from Othello's
11   mind!
12   EMILIA: Lady, amen.
13   DESDEMONA: I will go seek him. Cassio, walk here about.
14   If I do find him fit, I'll move your suit
15   And seek to effect it to my uttermost.
16   CASSIO: I humbly thank your ladyship. *(Exit DESDEMONA*
17   *and EMILIA. Enter BIANCA)*
18   BIANCA: Save you, friend Cassio!
19   CASSIO: What make you from home?
20   How is it with you, my most fair Bianca?
21   I' faith, sweet love, I was coming to your house.
22   BIANCA: And I was going to your lodging, Cassio.
23   What, keep a week away? seven days and nights?
24   Eightscore eight hours? and lovers' absent hours,
25   More tedious than the dial eightscore times?
26   O weary reck'ning!
27   CASSIO: Pardon me, Bianca.
28   I have this while with leaden thoughts been pressed;
29   But I shall in a more convenient time
30   Strike off this score of absence. Sweet Bianca, *(Gives her*
31   *Desdemona's handkerchief.)*
32   Take me this work out.
33   BIANCA: O Cassio, whence came this?
34   This is some token from a newer friend.
35   To the felt absence now I feel a cause.

1   Is't come to this? Well, well.

2 CASSIO: Go to, woman!

3   Throw your vile guesses in the devil's teeth,

4   From whence you have them. You are jealous now

5   That this is from some mistress, some remembrance.

6   No, by my faith, Bianca.

7 BIANCA: Why, whose is it?

8 CASSIO: I know not, sweet. I found it in my chamber.

9   I like the work well. Ere it be demanded,

10   As like enough it will, I would have it copied.

11   Take it and do't, and leave me for this time.

12 BIANCA: Leave you? Wherefore?

13 CASSIO: I do attend here on the General

14   And think it no addition, nor my wish,

15   To have him see me womaned.

16 BIANCA: Why, I pray you?

17 CASSIO: Not that I love you not.

18 BIANCA: But that you do not love me!

19   I pray you bring me on the way a little,

20   And say if I shall see you soon at night.

21 CASSIO: 'Tis but a little way that I can bring you,

22   For I attend here; but I'll see you soon.

23 BIANCA: 'Tis very good. I must be circumstanced. *(Exit*

24   *CASSIO and BIANCA)*

25

26

27

28

29

30

31

32

33

34

35

Hamlet
Act I, Scene 1

CHARACTERS

Bernardo, Horatio, Francisco, Marcellus — night watchmen at the castle of Elsinore

Ghost — spirit of Hamlet's father

The opening scene of this tragedy is most important because of its tone: the mood is dark, somber, and melancholy. It is at night at the royal castle at Elsinore, and four soldiers and officers are conversing about a strange and frightening apparition that had been seen during the previous nightwatch. Just as Bernardo tells Horatio how the ghost had appeared one hour after midnight, the Ghost itself enters. It is the spirit of the late King Hamlet of Denmark and appears in "warlike form." Marcellus insists that Horatio approach and question it, but, as he does so, the specter exits.

The ghost again appears, and again Horatio challenges it to speak. But, at the break of dawn (as signaled by the crowing of a rooster), it moves from one place to another and departs. All of the witnesses, however, agree that Hamlet, the son of this ghostly spirit, must be told.

We learn some interesting and essential elements from the conversation of Bernardo, Francisco, Horatio, and Marcellus. First of all, the Ghost has appeared twice before in the same armor King Hamlet wore when he fought Fortinbras, King of Norway, and slew him in battle. Now the dead king's son, young Fortinbras, is raising an army and is determined to take back the lands his father lost (thus the reason for the nightwatch at the castle of Elsinore).

It is also imperative to understand the importance of ghostly apparitions — the characters in this play, like most people of this time, fully believed in ghosts. The prevailing theories were that a ghost may be one of the following: a) an hallucination; b) a spirit returned to perform some deed left undone in life; c) a spirit returned from the grave by divine permission; d) a devil disguised as a dead person; or e) as an omen.

1	**SETTING:**	Elsinore. A platform before the castle.
2	**AT RISE:**	Francisco at his post. Enter to him Bernardo.
3		
4	**BERNARDO:**	Who's there?
5	**FRANCISCO:**	Nay, answer me: stand, and unfold yourself.
6	**BERNARDO:**	Long live the king!
7	**FRANCISCO:**	Bernardo?
8	**BERNARDO:**	He.
9	**FRANCISCO:**	You come most carefully upon your hour.
10	**BERNARDO:**	'Tis now struck twelve; get thee to bed,
11		Francisco.
12	**FRANCISCO:**	For this relief much thanks: 'tis bitter cold,
13		And I am sick at heart.
14	**BERNARDO:**	Have you had quiet guard?
15	**FRANCISCO:**	Not a mouse stirring.
16	**BERNARDO:**	Well, good night.
17		If you do meet Horatio and Marcellus,
18		The rivals of my watch, bid them make haste.
19	**FRANCISCO:**	I think I hear them. — Stand, ho! Who is there?
20		*(Enter HORATIO and MARCELLUS)*
21	**HORATIO:**	Friends to this ground.
22	**MARCELLUS:**	And liegemen to the Dane.
23	**FRANCISCO:**	Give you good night.
24	**MARCELLUS:**	O, farewell, honest soldier:
25		Who hath relieved you?
26	**FRANCISCO:**	Bernardo has my place.
27		Give you good night. *(Exit FRANCISCO)*
28	**MARCELLUS:**	Holla! Bernardo!
29	**BERNARDO:**	Say, —
30		What, is Horatio there?
31	**HORATIO:**	A piece of him.
32	**BERNARDO:**	Welcome, Horatio: — welcome, good Marcellus.
33	**MARCELLUS:**	What, has this thing appear'd again tonight?
34	**BERNARDO:**	I have seen nothing.
35	**MARCELLUS:**	Horatio says 'tis but our fantasy,

1   And will not let belief take hold of him

2   Touching this dreaded sight, twice seen of us:

3   Therefore I have entreated him along

4   With us to watch the minutes of this night;

5   That, if again this apparition come,

6   He may approve our eyes, and speak to it.

7   HORATIO: Tush, tush, 'twill not appear.

8   BERNARDO: Sit down awhile;

9   And let us once again assail your ears,

10   That are so fortified against our story,

11   What we two nights have seen.

12   HORATIO: Well, sit we down,

13   And let us hear Bernardo speak of this.

14   BERNARDO: Last night of all,

15   When yond same star that's westward from the pole

16   Had made his course t'illume that part of heaven

17   Where now it burns, Marcellus and myself,

18   The bell then beating one, —

19   MARCELLUS: Peace, break thee off; look, where it comes

20   again! *(Enter GHOST)*

21   BERNARDO: In the same figure, like the king that's dead.

22   MARCELLUS: Thou art a scholar; speak to it, Horatio.

23   BERNARDO: Looks it not like the king? mark it, Horatio.

24   HORATIO: Most like: — it harrows me with fear and wonder.

25   BERNARDO: It would be spoke to.

26   MARCELLUS: Question it, Horatio.

27   HORATIO: What art thou, that usurp'st this time of night,

28   Together with that fair and warlike form

29   In which the majesty of buried Denmark

30   Did sometimes march? by heaven I charge thee, speak!

31   MARCELLUS: It is offended.

32   BERNARDO: See, it stalks away!

33   HORATIO: Stay! speak, speak! I charge thee, speak! *(Exit*

34   *GHOST)*

35   MARCELLUS: 'Tis gone, and will not answer.

1   BERNARDO: How now, Horatio! you tremble, and look pale:
2   Is not this something more than fantasy?
3   What think you on't?
4   HORATIO: Before my God, I might not this believe
5   Without the sensible and true avouch
6   Of mine own eyes.
7   MARCELLUS: Is it not like the king?
8   HORATIO: As thou art to thyself:
9   Such was the very armour he had on
10   When he th'ambitious Norway combated;
11   So frown'd he once, when, in an angry parle,
12   He smote the sledded Polacks on the ice.
13   'Tis strange.
14   MARCELLUS: Thus twice before, and jump at this dead hour,
15   With martial stalk hath he gone by our watch.
16   HORATIO: In what particular thought to work I know not;
17   But, in the gross and scope of my opinion,
18   This bodes some strange eruption to our state.
19   MARCELLUS: Good now, sit down, and tell me, he that
20   knows,
21   Why this same strict and most observant watch
22   So nightly toils the subject of the land;
23   And why such daily cast of brazen cannon,
24   And foreign mart for implements of war;
25   Why such impress of shipwrights, whose sore task
26   Does not divide the Sunday from the week;
27   What might be toward, that this sweaty haste
28   Doth make the night joint-laborer with the day:
29   Who is't that can inform me?
30   HORATIO: That can I;
31   At least, the whisper goes so. Our last king,
32   Whose image even but now appear'd to us,
33   Was, as you know, by Fortinbras of Norway,
34   Thereto prickt on by a most emulate pride,
35   Dared to the combat; in which our valiant Hamlet —

1	For so this side of our known world esteem'd him —
2	Did slay this Fortinbras; who, by a seal'd compact,
3	Well ratified by law and heraldry,
4	Did forfeit, with his life, all those his lands
5	Which he stood seized of to the conqueror:
6	Against the which, a moiety competent
7	Was gaged by our king; which had return'd
8	To the inheritance of Fortinbras,
9	Had he been vanquisher; as, by the same cov'nant,
10	And carriage of the article design'd,
11	His fell to Hamlet. Now, sir, young Fortinbras,
12	Of unimproved mettle hot and full,
13	Hath in the skirts of Norway, here and there,
14	Sharkt up a list of lawless resolutes,
15	For food and diet, to some enterprise
16	That hath a stomach in't: which is no other —
17	As it doth well appear unto our state —
18	But to recover of us, by strong hand
19	And terms compulsative, those foresaid lands
20	So by his father lost: and this, I take it,
21	Is the main motive of our preparations,
22	The source of this our watch, and the chief head
23	Of this post-haste and romage¹ in the land.
24	BERNARDO: I think it be no other but e'en so:
25	Well may it sort that this portentous figure
26	Comes armed through our watch; so like the king
27	That was and is the question of these wars.
28	HORATIO: A mote it is to trouble the mind's eye.
29	In the most high and palmy state of Rome,
30	A little ere the mightiest Julius fell,
31	The graves stood tenantless, and the sheeted dead
32	Did squeak and gibber in the Roman streets:
33	As, stars with trains of fire and dews of blood,
34	
35	¹*romage: unrest.*

1   Disasters in the sun; and the moist star,
2   Upon whose influence Neptune's empire stands,
3   Was sick almost to doomsday with eclipse:
4   And even the like precurse of the fierce events —
5   As harbingers preceding still the fates,
6   And prologue to the omen coming on —
7   Have heaven and earth together demonstrated
8   Unto our climatures and countrymen. —
9   But soft, behold! lo, where it comes again! *(Enter GHOST*
10   *again)*
11   I'll cross it, though it blast me. — Stay, illusion!
12   If thou hast any sound, or use of voice,
13   Speak to me:
14   If there be any good thing to be done,
15   That may to thee do ease, and grace to me,
16   Speak to me:
17   If thou art privy to thy country's fate,
18   Which, happily, foreknowing may avoid,
19   O, speak!
20   Or if thou hast uphoarded in thy life
21   Extorted treasure in the womb of earth,
22   For which, they say, you spirits oft walk in death, *(Cock*
23   *crows.)*
24   Speak of it: — stay, and speak! — Stop it, Marcellus.
25 MARCELLUS: Shall I strike at it with my partisan?
26 HORATIO: Do, if it will not stand.
27 BERNARDO: 'Tis here!
28 HORATIO: 'Tis here!
29 MARCELLUS: 'Tis gone! *(Exit GHOST)*
30   We do it wrong, being so majestical,
31   To offer it the show of violence;
32   For it is, as the air, invulnerable,
33   And our vain blows malicious mockery.
34 BERNARDO: It was about to speak when the cock crew.
35 HORATIO: And then it started like a guilty thing

1   Upon a fearful summons. I have heard,

2   The cock, that is the trumpet to the morn,

3   Doth with his lofty and shrill-sounding throat

4   Awake the god of day; and at his warning,

5   Whether in sea or fire, in earth or air,

6   Th'extravagant and erring spirit hies

7   To his confine: and of the truth herein

8   This present object made probation.

9 MARCELLUS: It faded on the crowing of the cock.

10

11

12

13

14

15

16

17

18

19

20

21

22

23

24

25

26

27

28

29

30

31

32

33

34

35

Hamlet
Act I, Scene 2

MAJOR CHARACTERS

Claudius, King of Denmark — Hamlet's uncle who succeeded his brother to the throne and married his wife

Hamlet, Prince of Denmark — son of the dead King Hamlet and nephew to the present ruler of Denmark. He has returned to Elsinore because of his father's death.

MINOR CHARACTERS

Gertrude — Queen of Denmark and mother of Hamlet

Horatio — a loyal friend of Hamlet

EXTRAS — **Voltimand, Cornelius, Laertes, Polonius, Marcellus, Bernardo**

This scene takes place in a state room in the castle of Elsinore. Claudius, the new king of Denmark, enters with his new bride, Gertrude, and is accompanied by Lord Chamberlain Polonius and his son Laertes. It is important to understand what has recently occurred: Claudius' brother, King Hamlet, was recently killed in battle, and, in the short span of two months, Claudius has married his dead brother's wife and has become ruler of the land.

Understandably, Prince Hamlet, the dead king's son, is upset by this. Not only has his mother remarried within a time span of grief and mourning, but her marriage, according to canon law, is considered incestuous: her marriage to her brother-in-law was a gross violation of the law of the church. Furthermore, we are not given many clues to the reasoning behind Gertrude's motivations: did she marry quickly to keep the rule of the land intact, or, as Hamlet suggests in lines 12-14 on page 97, was it born from weakness manifested by sensual passion?

Nevertheless, Claudius recognizes Hamlet's anguish. It should be noted that Claudius is indeed a wise and astute man: he is fully aware that his marriage is incestuous and has taken place in haste, but he convinces his public that he is motivated by a high sense of duty. In the beginning of this scene, he speaks of mourning the death of his "dear brother" and explains that "discretion" prohibits excessive grief. Both Claudius and Gertrude speak to Hamlet about accepting his father's death philosophically and explain that the grief Hamlet feels is not unique; they then, however, urge Hamlet to end his grieving by saying that it is unmanly and reflects "impious stubbornness."

Alone, Hamlet expresses his innermost thoughts: he contemplates suicide, but it is strictly prohibited in God's law. Horatio, Hamlet's loyal friend, enters and explains that he has just returned from attending the funeral of Hamlet's father. Hamlet expresses his regret and anxiety at his mother's marriage to his uncle, and, suddenly, tells Horatio that he thinks he sees his dead father. Though Hamlet was speaking imaginatively, it does provide Horatio the opportunity to tell Hamlet that he and three other guards have seen the Ghost of Hamlet's father. After tense questioning, Hamlet concludes that the Ghost is an omen and that he must approach and confront it.

1 **SETTING:** A room of state in the castle.

2 **AT RISE:** Enter the King, Queen, Hamlet, Polonius, Laertes,

3   Voltimand, Cornelius, Lords, and Attendants.

4

5 KING: Though yet of Hamlet our dear brother's death

6   The memory be green; and that it us befitted

7   To bear our hearts in grief, and our whole kingdom

8   To be contracted in one brow of woe;

9   Yet so far hath discretion fought with nature,

10   That we with wisest sorrow think on him,

11   Together with remembrance of ourselves.

12   Therefore our sometime sister, now our queen,

13   Th'imperial jointress of this warlike state,

14   Have we, as 'twere with a defeated joy, —

15   With one auspicious, and one dropping eye,

16   With mirth in funeral, and with dirge in marriage,

17   In equal scale weighing delight and dole, —

18   Taken to wife: nor have we herein barr'd

19   Your better wisdoms, which have freely gone—

20   With this affair along: — for all, our thanks.

21   Now follows, that you know, young Fortinbras,

22   Holding a weak supposal of our worth,

23   Or thinking by our late dear brother's death

24   Our state to be disjoint and out of frame,

25   Colleagued with the dream of his advantage, —

26   He hath not fail'd to pester us with message,

27   Importing the surrender of those lands

28   Lost by his father, with all bands of law,

29   To our most valiant brother. So much for him. —

30   Now for ourself, and for this time of meeting:

31   Thus much the business is: — we have here writ

32   To Norway, uncle of young Fortinbras, —

33   Who, impotent and bed-rid, scarcely hears

34   Of this his nephew's purpose, — to suppress

35   His further gait herein, in that the levies,

1   The lists, and full proportions, are all made
2   Out of his subject: — and we here dispatch
3   You, good Cornelius, and you, Voltimand,
4   For bearers of this greeting to old Norway;
5   Giving to you no further personal power
6   To business with the king, more than the scope
7   Of these delated articles allow.
8   Farewell; and let your haste commend your duty.
9   CORNELIUS and VOLTIMAND: In that and all things will
10   we show our duty.
11   KING: We doubt it nothing: heartily farewell. *(Exit VOLTIMAND*
12   *and CORNELIUS)*
13   And now, Laertes, what's the news with you?
14   You told us of some suit; what is't, Laertes?
15   You cannot speak of reason to the Dane,
16   And lose your voice: what would'st thou beg, Laertes,
17   That shall not be my offer, not thy asking?
18   The head is not more native to the heart,
19   The hand more instrumental to the mouth,
20   Than is the throne of Denmark to thy father.
21   What wouldst thou have, Laertes?
22   LAERTES: My dread lord,
23   Your leave and favor to return to France;
24   From whence though willingly I came to Denmark,
25   To show my duty in your coronation;
26   Yet now, I must confess, that duty done,
27   My thoughts and wishes bend again toward France,
28   And bow them to your gracious leave and pardon.
29   KING: Have you your father's leave? What says Polonius?
30   POLONIUS: He hath, my lord, wrung from me my slow leave
31   By laborsome petition; and, at last,
32   Upon his will I seal'd my hard consent:
33   I do beseech you, give him leave to go.
34   KING: Take thy fair hour, Laertes; time be thine,
35   And thy best graces spend it at thy will! —

1   But now, my cousin Hamlet, and my son, —
2   HAMLET: *(Aside)* A little more than kin, and less than kind.
3   KING: How is it that the clouds still hang on you?
4   HAMLET: Not so, my lord; I am too much i'th'sun.
5   QUEEN: Good Hamlet, cast thy nighted color off,
6   And let thine eye look like a friend on Denmark.
7   Do not for ever with thy vailed lids
8   Seek for thy noble father in the dust:
9   Thou know'st 'tis common, — all that live must die,
10   Passing through nature to eternity.
11 HAMLET: Ay, madam, it is common.
12 QUEEN: If it be,
13   Why seems it so particular with thee?
14 HAMLET: Seems, madam! nay, it is; I know not "seems."
15   'Tis not alone my inky cloak, good mother,
16   Nor customary suits of solemn black,
17   Nor windy suspiration of forced breath,
18   No, nor the fruitful river in the eye,
19   Nor the dejected havior of the visage,
20   Together with all forms, moods, shows of grief,
21   That can denote me truly: these, indeed, seem,
22   For they are actions that a man might play:
23   But I have that within which passeth show;
24   These but the trappings and the suits of woe.
25 KING: 'Tis sweet and commendable in your nature, Hamlet,
26   To give these mourning duties to your father:
27   But, you must know, your father lost a father;
28   That father lost, lost his; and the survivor bound,
29   In filial obligation, for some term
30   To do obsequious sorrow: but to persever
31   In obstinate condolement, is a course
32   Of impious stubbornness, tis unmanly grief:
33   It shows a will most incorrect to heaven,
34   A heart unfortified, a mind impatient;
35   An understanding simple and unschool'd:

1 For what we know must be, and is as common
2 As any the most vulgar thing to sense,
3 Why should we, in our peevish opposition,
4 Take it to heart? Fie! 'tis a fault to heaven,
5 A fault against the dead, a fault to nature,
6 To reason most absurd; whose common theme
7 Is death of fathers, and who still hath cried,
8 From the first corse till he that died today,
9 "This must be so." We pray you, throw to earth
10 This unprevailing woe; and think of us
11 As of a father: for let the world take note,
12 You are the most immediate to our throne;
13 And with no less nobility of love
14 Than that which dearest father bears his son,
15 Do I impart toward you. For your intent
16 In going back to school in Wittenberg,
17 It is most retrograde to our desire:
18 And we beseech you, bend you to remain
19 Here, in the cheer and comfort of our eye,
20 Our chiefest courtier, cousin, and our son.
21 QUEEN: Let not thy mother lose her prayers, Hamlet:
22 I pray thee, stay with us; go not to Wittenberg.
23 HAMLET: I shall in all my best obey you, madam.
24 KING: Why, 'tis a loving and a fair reply:
25 Be as ourself in Denmark. — Madam, come;
26 This gentle and unforced accord of Hamlet
27 Sits smiling to my heart: in grace whereof,
28 No jocund health that Denmark drinks today,
29 But the great cannon to the clouds shall tell;
30 And the king's rouse the heaven shall bruit again,
31 Re-speaking earthly thunder. Come away. *(Exit all but*
32 *HAMLET)*
33 HAMLET: O, that this too too solid flesh would melt,
34 Thaw, and resolve itself into a dew!
35 Or that the Everlasting had not fixt

1   His canon 'gainst self-slaughter! O God! God!

2   How weary, stale, flat, and unprofitable

3   Seem to me all the uses of this world!

4   Fie on't! O, fie! 'tis an unweeded garden,

5   That grows to seed; things rank and gross in nature

6   Possess it merely. That it should come to this!

7   But two months dead! — nay, not so much, not two:

8   So excellent a king; that was, to this,

9   Hyperion to a satyr: so loving to my mother,

10   That he might not beteem the winds of heaven

11   Visit her face too roughly. Heaven and earth!

12   Must I remember? why, she would hang on him,

13   As if increase of appetite had grown

14   By what it fed on: and yet, within a month, —

15   Let me not think on't, — Frailty, thy name is woman! —

16   A little month; or e'er those shoes were old

17   With which she follow'd my poor father's body,

18   Like Niobe, all tears; — why she, even she —

19   O God! a beast, that wants discourse of reason,

20   Would have mourn'd longer — married with my uncle,

21   My father's brother; but no more like my father

22   Than I to Hercules; within a month;

23   Ere yet the salt of most unrighteous tears

24   Had left the flushing in her galled eyes,

25   She married: — O, most wicked speed, to post

26   With such dexterity to incestuous sheets!

27   It is not nor it cannot come to good:

28   But break, my heart, — for I must hold my tongue! *(Enter*

29   *HORATIO, MARCELLUS, and BERNARDO)*

30 HORATIO: Hail to your lordship!

31 HAMLET: I am glad to see you well:

32   Horatio, — or I do forget myself.

33 HORATIO: The same, my lord, and your poor servant ever.

34 HAMLET: Sir, my good friend; I'll change that name with you:

35   And what make you from Wittenberg, Horatio? —

1	Marcellus?
2	MARCELLUS: My good lord, —
3	HAMLET: I am very glad to see you. — Good even, sir. —
4	But what, in faith, make you from Wittenberg?
5	HORATIO: A truant disposition, good my lord.
6	HAMLET: I would not hear your enemy say so;
7	Nor shall you do mine ear that violence
8	To make it truster of your own report
9	Against yourself: I know you are no truant.
10	But what is your affair in Elsinore?
11	We'll teach you to drink deep ere you depart.
12	HORATIO: My lord, I came to see your father's funeral.
13	HAMLET: I pray thee, do not mock me, fellow-student;
14	I think it was to see my mother's wedding.
15	HORATIO: Indeed, my lord, it follow'd hard upon.
16	HAMLET: Thrift, thrift, Horatio! the funeral baked meats
17	Did coldly furnish forth the marriage tables.
18	Would I had met my dearest foe in heaven
19	Or ever I had seen that day, Horatio! —
20	My father, — methinks I see my father.
21	HORATIO: O, where, my lord?
22	HAMLET: In my mind's eye, Horatio.
23	HORATIO: I saw him once; he was a goodly king.
24	HAMLET: He was a man, take him for all in all,
25	I shall not look upon his like again.
26	HORATIO: My lord, I think I saw him yesternight.
27	HAMLET: Saw? who?
28	HORATIO: My lord, the king your father.
29	HAMLET: The king my father!
30	HORATIO: Season your admiration for a while
31	With an attent ear; till I may deliver,
32	Upon the witness of these gentlemen,
33	This marvel to you.
34	HAMLET: For God's love, let me hear.
35	HORATIO: Two nights together had these gentlemen,

1   Marcellus and Bernardo, on their watch,
2   In the dead vast and middle of the night,
3   Been thus encounter'd. A figure like your father,
4   Armed at point, exactly, cap-a-pe. [1]
5   Appears before them, and with solemn march
6   Goes slowly and stately by them: thrice he walkt
7   By their opprest and fear-surprised eyes,
8   Within his truncheon's length; whilst they, distill'd
9   Almost to jelly with the act of fear,
10   Stand dumb, and speak not to him. This to me
11   In dreadful secrecy impart they did;
12   And I with them the third night kept the watch:
13   Where, as they had deliver'd, both in time,
14   Form of the thing, each word made true and good,
15   The apparition comes: I knew your father;
16   These hands are not more like.
17   HAMLET: But where was this?
18   MARCELLUS: My lord, upon the platform where we watcht.
19   HAMLET: Did you not speak to it?
20   HORATIO: My lord, I did;
21   But answer made it none: yet once methought
22   It lifted up its head and did address
23   Itself to motion, like as it would speak:
24   But even then the morning cock crew loud;
25   And at the sound it shrunk in haste away,
26   And vanisht from our sight.
27   HAMLET: 'Tis very strange.
28   HORATIO: As I do live, my honour'd lord, 'tis true;
29   And we did think it writ down in our duty
30   To let you know of it.
31   HAMLET: Indeed, indeed, sirs, but this troubles me.
32   Hold you the watch tonight?
33   MARCELLUS and BERNARDO: We do, my lord.
34
35   [1] *cap-a-pe: from head to foot.*

1	**HAMLET:** Arm'd, say you?
2	**MARCELLUS and BERNARDO:** Arm'd, my lord.
3	**HAMLET:** From top to toe?
4	**MARCELLUS and BERNARDO:** My lord, from head to foot.
5	**HAMLET:** Then saw you not his face?
6	**HORATIO:** O, yes, my lord; he wore his beaver¹ up.
7	**HAMLET:** What, lookt he frowningly?
8	**HORATIO:** A countenance more in sorrow than in anger.
9	**HAMLET:** Pale or red?
10	**HORATIO:** Nay, very pale.
11	**HAMLET:** And fixt his eyes upon you?
12	**HORATIO:** Most constantly.
13	**HAMLET:** I would I had been there.
14	**HORATIO:** It would have much amazed you.
15	**HAMLET:** Very like, very like. Stay'd it long?
16	**HORATIO:** While one with moderate haste might tell a
17	hundred.
18	**MARCELLUS and BERNARDO:** Longer, longer.
19	**HORATIO:** Not when I saw't.
20	**HAMLET:** His beard was grizzled, — no?
21	**HORATIO:** It was, as I have seen it in his life,
22	A sable silver'd.
23	**HAMLET:** I will watch tonight;
24	Perchance 'twill walk again.
25	**HORATIO:** I warrant it will.
26	**HAMLET:** If it assume my noble father's person,
27	I'll speak to it, though hell itself should gape,
28	And bid me hold my peace. I pray you all,
29	If you have hitherto conceal'd this sight,
30	Let it be tenable in your silence still;
31	And whatsoever else shall hap tonight,
32	Give it an understanding, but no tongue:
33	I will requite your loves. So, fare you well:
34	
35	¹*beaver: visor.*

1   Upon the platform, 'twixt eleven and twelve,
2   I'll visit you.
3 ALL: Our duty to your honor.
4 HAMLET: Your loves, as mine to you: farewell. *(Exit all but*
5   *HAMLET)*
6   My father's spirit in arms! all is not well;
7   I doubt some foul play: would the night were come!
8   Till then sit still, my soul: foul deeds will rise,
9   Though all the earth o'erwhelm them to men's eyes. *(He*
10   *exits.)*
11
12
13
14
15
16
17
18
19
20
21
22
23
24
25
26
27
28
29
30
31
32
33
34
35

Hamlet
Act I, Scene 5

MAJOR CHARACTERS

Hamlet — Prince of Denmark

Ghost — the spirit of Hamlet's dead father

MINOR CHARACTERS

Horatio — loyal friend to Hamlet

EXTRA — **Marcellus**

For Hamlet, this scene is one of confrontation and of confirmation: it is the first time in the play that Hamlet actually approaches and questions the Ghost of his deceased father (although earlier in the play he does see it); furthermore, his suspicions about his murderous uncle are confirmed.

To begin, the Ghost tells Hamlet that he is doomed to walk on earth during the nights and suffer the purgatorial fires for sins he committed during his lifetime; we therefore realize that the Ghost is aware of mortal imperfections and has a strict moral conscience. However, the Ghost asks Hamlet to seek revenge for his murder and to prove his love for his father. He tells Hamlet that he was murdered by Claudius, "that incestuous, that adulterate beast," who, while King Hamlet slept, poured poison into his ear, sending him to his death.

The two major elements to Hamlet's tragedy are now joined: the murder of a king and father, and the incestuous marriage of his uncle to his mother. In a state of great excitement, Hamlet declares revenge. He swears an oath of secrecy with his two friends, Horatio and Marcellus, and admonishes them that if he chooses to pretend to be mentally deranged, they are not to give the slightest indication that they know the reason for his behavior. (It must be noted that the Ghost specifically requests Hamlet to not punish his mother; he is to leave her punishment to heaven and to her own conscience.)

Lines 9-10 on page 109 fully encompass the enormous task Hamlet has before him:
"The time is out of joint; — O cursed spite,
That ever I was born to set it right."

1 *SETTING:* Another part of the platform.
2 *AT RISE:* Enter Ghost and Hamlet.
3
4 HAMLET: Where wilt thou lead me? speak; I'll go no further.
5 GHOST: Mark me.
6 HAMLET: I will.
7 GHOST: My hour is almost come,
8   When I to sulphurous and tormenting flames
9   Must render up myself.
10 HAMLET: Alas, poor ghost!
11 GHOST: Pity me not, but lend thy serious hearing
12   To what I shall unfold.
13 HAMLET: Speak; I am bound to hear.
14 GHOST: So art thou to revenge, when thou shalt hear.
15 HAMLET: What?
16 GHOST: I am thy father's spirit;
17   Doom'd for a certain term to walk the night,
18   And for the day confined to fast in fires,
19   Till the foul crimes done in my days of nature
20   Are burnt and purged away. But that I am forbid
21   To tell the secrets of my prison-house,
22   I could a tale unfold, whose lightest word
23   Would harrow up thy soul; freeze thy young blood;
24   Make thy two eyes, like stars, start from their spheres;
25   Thy knotted and combined locks to part,
26   And each particular hair to stand an end,
27   Like quills upon the fretful porpentine:
28   But this eternal blazon must not be
29   To ears of flesh and blood. — List, list, O, list! —
30   If thou didst ever thy dear father love, —
31 HAMLET: O God!
32 GHOST: Revenge his foul and most unnatural murder.
33 HAMLET: Murder!
34 GHOST: Murder most foul, as in the best it is;
35   But this most foul, strange, and unnatural.

1   HAMLET: Haste me to know't, that I, with wings as swift

2   As meditation or the thoughts of love,

3   May sweep to my revenge.

4   GHOST: I find thee apt;

5   And duller shouldst thou be than the fat weed

6   That roots itself in ease on Lethe wharf,

7   Wouldst thou not stir in this. Now, Hamlet, hear:

8   'Tis given out that, sleeping in my orchard,

9   A serpent stung me; so the whole ear of Denmark

10   Is by a forged process of my death

11   Rankly abused: but know, thou noble youth,

12   The serpent that did sting thy father's life

13   Now wears his crown.

14   HAMLET: O my prophetic soul!

15   My uncle!

16   GHOST: Ay, that incestuous, that adulterate beast,

17   With witchcraft of his wit, with traitorous gifts, —

18   O wicked wit and gifts, that have the power

19   So to seduce! — won to his shameful lust

20   The will of my most seeming-virtuous queen:

21   O Hamlet, what a falling-off was there!

22   From me, whose love was of that dignity,

23   That it went hand in hand even with the vow

24   I made to her in marriage; and to decline

25   Upon a wretch, whose natural gifts were poor

26   To those of mine!

27   But virtue, as it never will be moved,

28   Though lewdness court it in a shape of heaven;

29   So lust, though to a radiant angel linkt,

30   Will sate itself in a celestial bed,

31   And prey on garbage.

32   But, soft! methinks I scent the morning air;

33   Brief let me be. — Sleeping within my orchard,

34   My custom always in the afternoon,

35   Upon my secure hour thy uncle stole,

1	With juice of cursed hebenon in a vial,
2	And in the porches of mine ears did pour
3	The leperous distilment; whose effect
4	Holds such an enmity with blood of man,
5	That, swift as quicksilver, it courses through
6	The natural gates and alleys of the body;
7	And, with a sudden vigour, it doth posset
8	And curd, like eager droppings into milk,
9	The thin and wholesome blood: so did it mine;
10	And a most instant tetter barkt about,[1]
11	Most lazar-like, with vile and loathsome crust
12	All my smooth body.
13	Thus was I, sleeping, by a brother's hand
14	Of life, of crown, of queen, at once dispatcht:
15	Cut off even in the blossoms of my sin,
16	Unhousell'd, disappointed, unaneled;
17	No reckoning made, but sent to my account
18	With all my imperfections on my head:
19	O, horrible! O, horrible! most horrible!
20	If thou hast nature in thee, bear it not;
21	Let not the royal bed of Denmark be
22	A couch for luxury and damned incest.
23	But, howsoever thou pursuest this act,
24	Taint not thy mind, nor let thy soul contrive
25	Against thy mother aught: leave her to heaven,
26	And to those thorns that in her bosom lodge
27	To prick and sting her. Fare thee well at once!
28	The glow-worm shows the matin to be near,
29	And 'gins to pale his uneffectual fire:
30	Adieu, adieu, adieu! remember me. *(Exit GHOST)*
31	HAMLET: O all you host of heaven! O earth! what else?
32	And shall I couple hell? — O, fie! — Hold, hold, my heart;
33	And you, my sinews, grow not instant old,
34	
35	[1] *tetter barkt about: covered with sores.*

1   But bear me stiffly up. — Remember thee!
2   Ay, thou poor ghost, while memory holds a seat
3   In this distracted globe. Remember thee!
4   Yea, from the table of my memory
5   I'll wipe away all trivial fond records,
6   All saws[1] of books, all forms, all pressures past,
7   That youth and observation copied there;
8   And thy commandment all alone shall live
9   Within the book and volume of my brain,
10 Unmixt with baser matter: yes, by heaven! —
11 O most pernicious woman!
12 O villain, villain, smiling, damned villain!
13 My tables, — meet it is I set it down,
14 That one may smile, and smile, and be a villain;
15 At least I'm sure it may be so in Denmark: *(Writing)*
16 So, uncle, there you are. Now to my word;
17 It is, "Adieu, adieu! remember me:"
18 I have sworn't.
19 HORATIO: *(Within)* My lord, my lord, —
20 MARCELLUS: *(Within)* Lord Hamlet, —
21 HORATIO: *(Within)* Heaven secure him!
22 HAMLET: So be it!
23 HORATIO: *(Within)* Illo, ho, ho, my lord!
24 HAMLET: Hillo, ho, ho, boy! come, bird, come. *(Enter*
25   *HORATIO and MARCELLUS)*
26 MARCELLUS: How is't, my noble lord?
27 HORATIO: What news, my lord?
28 HAMLET: O, wonderful!
29 HORATIO: Good my lord, tell it.
30 HAMLET: No; you will reveal it.
31 HORATIO: Not I, my lord, by heaven.
32 MARCELLUS: Nor I, my lord.
33 HAMLET: How say you, then; would heart of man once think
34
35 [1]*saws: stories.*

1   it? —
2   But you'll be secret?
3 HORATIO and MARCELLUS: Ay by heaven, my lord.
4 HAMLET: There's ne'er a villain dwelling in all Denmark
5   But he's an arrant knave.
6 HORATIO: There needs no ghost, my lord, come from the
7   grave
8   To tell us this.
9 HAMLET: Why, right; you are i'th'right;
10   And so, without more circumstance at all,
11   I hold it fit that we shake hands and part:
12   You, as your business and desire shall point you, —
13   For every man hath business and desire,
14   Such as it is; — and for mine own poor part,
15   Look you, I'll go pray.
16 HORATIO: These are but wild and whirling words, my lord.
17 HAMLET: I'm sorry they offend you, heartily;
18   Yes, faith, heartily.
19 HORATIO: There's no offence, my lord.
20 HAMLET: Yes, by Saint Patrick, but there is, Horatio,
21   And much offence too. Touching this vision here, —
22   It is an honest ghost, that let me tell you:
23   For your desire to know what is between us,
24   O'ermaster't as you may. And now, good friends,
25   As you are friends, scholars, and soldiers,
26   Give me one poor request.
27 HORATIO: What is't, my lord? we will.
28 HAMLET: Never make known what you have seen tonight.
29 HORATIO and MARCELLUS: My lord, we will not.
30 HAMLET: Nay, but swear't.
31 HORATIO: In faith,
32   My lord, not I.
33 MARCELLUS: Nor I, my lord, in faith.
34 HAMLET: Upon my sword.
35 MARCELLUS: We have sworn, my lord, already.

1	HAMLET: Indeed, upon my sword, indeed.
2	GHOST: Swear! *(GHOST cries under the stage.)*
3	HAMLET: Ha, ha, boy! say'st thou so? Art thou there,
4	truepenny?
5	Come on; you hear this fellow in the cellarage;
6	Consent to swear.
7	HORATIO: Propose the oath, my lord.
8	HAMLET: Never to speak of this that you have seen.
9	Swear by my sword.
10	GHOST: *(Beneath)* Swear.
11	HAMLET: *Hic et ubique?* Then we'll shift our ground.
12	Come hither, gentlemen,
13	And lay your hands again upon my sword:
14	Swear by my sword
15	Never to speak of this that you have heard.
16	GHOST: *(Beneath)* Swear by his sword.
17	HAMLET: Well said, old mole! Canst work i'th' earth so fast?
18	A worthy pioner! Once more remove, good friends.
19	HORATIO: O day and night, but this is wondrous strange!
20	HAMLET: And therefore as a stranger give it welcome.
21	There are more things in heaven and earth, Horatio,
22	Than are dreamt of in your philosophy.
23	But come;
24	Here, as before, never, so help you mercy,
25	How strange or odd some'er I hear myself, —
26	As I perchance hereafter shall think meet
27	To put an antic disposition on —
28	That you, at such times seeing me, never shall,
29	With arms encumber'd thus, or this headshake,
30	Or by pronouncing of some doubtful phrase
31	As "Well, well we know," or "We could, an if we would,"
32	Or "If we list to speak," or "There be, an if they might,"
33	Or such ambiguous giving out, to note
34	That you know aught of me, — this do swear,
35	So grace and mercy at your most need help you.

1   **GHOST:** *(Beneath)* **Swear.**
2   **HAMLET: Rest, rest, perturbed spirit!** *(They swear.)* **So,**
3   gentlemen,
4   With all my love I do commend me to you;
5   And what so poor a man as Hamlet is
6   May do, t' express his love and friending to you,
7   God willing, shall not lack. Let us go in together;
8   And still your fingers on your lips, I pray.
9   The time is out of joint; O cursed spite,
10   That ever I was born to set it right!
11   Nay, come, let's go together. *(All exit.)*
12
13
14
15
16
17
18
19
20
21
22
23
24
25
26
27
28
29
30
31
32
33
34
35

Hamlet
Act III, Scene 1

(beginning with Hamlet's famous soliloquy)

MAJOR CHARACTERS

Hamlet — Prince of Denmark

Ophelia — daughter of Polonius, sister of Laertes, and the young lady who hopes to become Hamlet's bride

MINOR CHARACTERS

King Claudius — Hamlet's uncle who murdered Hamlet's father and married his mother

Polonius — counsel and friend to King Claudius

It is at this point in the play that Hamlet ponders his fate and the enormous task that his father's Ghost has requested: to avenge the murder of Hamlet's father by his brother Claudius.

It is discovered in earlier scenes that Hamlet's father, the recent King of Denmark, was poisoned by his brother Claudius; furthermore, Claudius married Hamlet's mother, Gertrude, within a two-month period after King Hamlet's death. The Ghost of Hamlet's father has returned, asking Hamlet to "revenge his foul and most unnatural murder."

Hamlet is at a crossroads: not only must he avenge his father's murder, but he is sickened by his mother's incestuous marriage to his uncle. He has been warned by the Ghost, however, to not harm his mother but allow her punishment to be dictated by heaven and the forces of her own conscience.

Claudius is aware that Hamlet is behaving oddly and is not to be trusted. Wise and shrewd, he watches Hamlet and warns Polonius, his chief counsel, of Hamlet's destructive potential. To gain more insight into the character of Hamlet and his brooding emotions, Polonius devises a plan: his daughter, Ophelia, to whom Hamlet has confessed his love, is to appear to be reading a book of devotions so that the Prince will not suspect her purpose; meanwhile, King Claudius and Polonius will be nearby listening to any confession or plan that Hamlet may put into action against them. (This action begins Scene 1 of Act III; however, the dialog has been omitted intentionally. As an in-class project, it is easiest to begin with Hamlet's famous soliloquy rather than assign the many parts with few lines in the scene's beginning.)

Thus, Hamlet ponders the question of "to be or not to be" when faced with great difficulties and tribulations. At the sight of Ophelia, he is aroused from his meditation; assuming that she is reading from the book of devotions, he urges her to pray for him.

In his melancholy state, his confusion, and his despair, he denies that he ever loved her, despite whatever he has said in the past. He declares that all men are "arrant knaves" and that none should be trusted. Before he exits, he says that she should seek haven in a nunnery and that any marriage for her will be catastrophic.

Alone, Ophelia expresses her profound sorrow of not only losing the love of her life, but she expresses grief that the once noble and virtuous mind and heart of Hamlet is forever gone.

1   **SETTING:**   Elsinore. A room in the castle.

2   **AT RISE:**   Ophelia is seated, appearing to read a devotion book.

3   Enter Hamlet.

4

5   HAMLET: To be, or not to be, — that is the question: —

6   Whether 'tis nobler in the mind to suffer

7   The slings and arrows of outrageous fortune,

8   Or to take arms against a sea of troubles,

9   And by opposing end them? — To die, — to sleep, —

10   No more; and by a sleep to say we end

11   The heart-ache, and the thousand natural shocks

12   That flesh is heir to, 'tis a consummation

13   Devoutly to be wisht. To die, — to sleep; —

14   To sleep! perchance to dream: ay, there's the rub;

15   For in that sleep of death what dreams may come,

16   When we have shuffled off this mortal coil,

17   Must give us pause: there's the respect

18   That makes calamity of so long life;

19   For who would bear the whips and scorns of time,

20   The oppressor's wrong, the proud man's contumely, [1]

21   The pangs of despised love, the law's delay,

22   The insolence of office, and the spurns

23   That patient merit of the unworthy takes,

24   When he himself might his quietus make

25   With a bare bodkin? [2] who would fardels [3] bear,

26   To grunt and sweat under a weary life,

27   But that the dread of something after death, —

28   The undiscover'd country, from whose bourn [4]

29   No traveller returns, — puzzles the will,

30   And makes us rather bear those ills we have

31

32   [1]*contumely: insult.*

33   [2]*bodkin: dagger.*

34   [3]*fardels: burdens.*

35   [4]*bourn: boundary.*

1   Than fly to others that we know not of?

2   Thus conscience does make cowards of us all;

3   And thus the native hue of resolution

4   Is sicklied o'er with the pale cast of thought;

5   And enterprises of great pith and moment,

6   With this regard, their currents turn awry,

7   And lose the name of action. — Soft you now!

8   The fair Ophelia! — Nymph, in thy orisons[1]

9   Be all my sins remember'd.

10   OPHELIA: Good my lord,

11   How does your honor for this many a day?

12   HAMLET: I humbly thank you; well, well, well.

13   OPHELIA: My lord, I have remembrances of yours,

14   That I have longed long to re-deliver;

15   I pray you, now receive them.

16   HAMLET: No, not I;

17   I never gave you aught.

18   OPHELIA: My honor'd lord, you know right well you did;

19   And, with them, words of so sweet breath composed

20   As made the things more rich: their perfume lost,

21   Take these again; for to the noble mind

22   Rich gifts wax poor when givers prove unkind.

23   There, my lord.

24   HAMLET: Ha, ha! are you honest?

25   OPHELIA: My lord?

26   HAMLET: Are you fair?

27   OPHELIA: What means your lordship?

28   HAMLET: That if you be honest and fair, your honesty should

29   admit no discourse to your beauty.

30   OPHELIA: Could beauty, my lord, have better commerce

31   than with honesty?

32   HAMLET: Ay, truly; for the power of beauty will sooner

33   transform honesty from what it is to a bawd than the force

34

35   [1]*orisons: prayers.*

1   of honesty can translate beauty into his likeness: this was
2   sometime a paradox, but now the time gives it proof. I did
3   love you once.
4   OPHELIA: Indeed, my lord, you made me believe so.
5   HAMLET: You should not have believed me; for virtue cannot
6   so inoculate our old stock, but we shall relish of it: I loved
7   you not.
8   OPHELIA: I was the more deceived.
9   HAMLET: Get thee to a nunnery: why wouldst thou be a
10   breeder of sinners? I am myself indifferent honest: but yet
11   I could accuse me of such things, that it were better my
12   mother had not borne me: I am very proud, revengeful,
13   ambitious; with more offences at my beck than I have
14   thoughts to put them in, imagination to give them shape,
15   or time to act them in. What should such fellows as I do
16   crawling between earth and heaven? We are arrant
17   knaves, all; believe none of us. Go thy ways to a nunnery.
18   Where's your father?
19   OPHELIA: At home, my lord.
20   HAMLET: Let the doors be shut upon him, that he may play
21   the fool no where but in's own house. Farewell.
22   OPHELIA: O, help him, you sweet heavens!
23   HAMLET: If thou dost marry, I'll give thee this plague for thy
24   dowry, — be thou as chaste as ice, as pure as snow, thou
25   shalt not escape calumny.[1] Get thee to a nunnery, go:
26   farewell. Or, if thou wilt needs marry, marry a fool; for
27   wise men know well enough what monsters you make of
28   them. To a nunnery, go; and quickly too. Farewell.
29   OPHELIA: O heavenly powers, restore him!
30   HAMLET: I have heard of your paintings too, well enough;
31   God has given you one face, and you make yourselves
32   another: you jig, you amble, and you lisp, and nickname
33   God's creatures, and make your wantonness your
34

35   [1]*calumny: gossip.*

1   ignorance. Go to, I'll no more on't; it hath made me mad.
2   I say, we will have no more marriages: those that are
3   married already, all but one, shall live; the rest shall keep
4   as they are. To a nunnery, go. *(Exit HAMLET)*
5 OPHELIA: O, what a noble mind is here o'erthrown!
6   The courtier's, soldier's, scholar's eye, tongue, sword;
7   Th'expectancy and rose of the fair state,
8   The glass of fashion and the mould of form,
9   Th'observ'd of all observers, — quite, quite down!
10   And I, of ladies most dejected and wretched,
11   That suckt the honey of his music vows,
12   Now see that noble and most sovereign reason,
13   Like sweet bells jangled, out of tune and harsh;
14   That unmatcht form and feature of blown youth
15   Blasted with ecstasy:[1] O, woe is me
16   T'have seen what I have seen, see what I see! *(Enter KING*
17   *and POLONIUS)*
18 KING: Love! his affections do not that way tend;
19   Nor what he spake, though it lackt form a little,
20   Was not like madness. There's something in his soul
21   O'er which his melancholy sits on brood;
22   And I do doubt the hatch and the disclose[2]
23   Will be some danger: which for to prevent,
24   I have in quick determination
25   Thus set it down: — he shall with speed to England,
26   For the demand of our neglected tribute:
27   Haply,[3] the seas, and countries different,
28   With variable objects, shall expel
29   This something settled matter in his heart;
30   Whereon his brains still beating puts him thus
31   From fashion of himself. What think you on't?
32
33 [1] *ecstasy: insanity.*
34 [2] *disclose: outcome.*
35 [3] *haply: maybe*

```
1    POLONIUS:   It shall do well: but yet do I believe
2           The origin and commencement of his grief
3           Sprung from neglected love. — How now, Ophelia!
4           You need not tell us what Lord Hamlet said;
5           We heard it all. — My lord, do as you please;
6           But, if you hold it fit, after the play,
7           Let his queen mother all alone entreat him
8           To show his grief: let her be round with him;
9           And I'll be placed, so please you, in the ear
10          Of all their conference. If she find him not,
11          To England send him; or confine him where
12          Your wisdom best shall think.
13   KING:   It shall be so:
14          Madness in great ones must not unwatcht go. (All exit.)
15
16
17
18
19
20
21
22
23
24
25
26
27
28
29
30
31
32
33
34
35
```

Hamlet
Act III, Scene 4

MAJOR CHARACTERS

Hamlet — Prince of Denmark

Gertrude — Hamlet's mother, Queen of Denmark

MINOR CHARACTERS

Polonius — counsel and friend to King Claudius, present King of Denmark and Hamlet's uncle

Ghost — spirit of Hamlet's dead father

Hamlet is melancholy. As shown in earlier scenes, Hamlet's father was murdered by his uncle Claudius. (He poured poison in his ear while he slept.) To make matters worse, he married Hamlet's mother, Gertrude, a mere two months after King Hamlet's death; therefore, it is not only his father's murder that anguishes him, it is the fact that his mother has married his uncle and is involved in an incestuous marriage, a relationship that not only angers and disgusts Hamlet but one that is against canon law.

In Act I, Scene 5, the Ghost of Hamlet's father appears. He not only tells Hamlet how Claudius murdered him, but he requests Hamlet to avenge his death. Hamlet swears to secrecy and to seek revenge.

Meanwhile, Claudius becomes suspect to Hamlet's melancholy behavior. He is aware that Hamlet still grieves over the death of his father, but he is also aware that Hamlet has enormous destructive potential. He and his counsel, Polonius, team together to watch, observe, and, ultimately, try and control Hamlet.

In this scene, Polonius is hiding behind the draperies in the Queen's chamber; he has insisted that Gertrude speak to her son about his behavior and his brooding mood. Gertrude begins firmly to reprove Hamlet, but, in his anger, he verbally takes the offensive. This frightens the Queen and causes her to call for help; and, from behind the draperies, Polonius echoes her cry. Quickly and angrily, Hamlet draws his sword and thrusts it through the curtain. "Is it the King?" he asks his distraught mother.

Hamlet begins then to interrogate his mother. He questions her reasons for marrying his uncle, and he contrasts the greatness of his father to the "mildew'd ear" of his uncle. The tormented Gertrude implores him to speak no more.

Suddenly, the Ghost of Hamlet's father appears, but only Hamlet sees it. Gertrude is convinced that her son is victim of a hallucination and has lost his mind. Hamlet replies gently to his mother that he is not mad; he also begs her to acknowledge her guilt, confess herself to heaven, and assume a virtue by avoiding further co-habitation with Claudius.

Hamlet's many moods are shown here. He is obedient, defiant, offensive, explosive, depressed, gentle, and virtuous. His moods are further contrasted when he callously states that he will remove Polonius' body: "I'll lug the guts into the neighbor room."

1   **SETTING:**   The Queen's closet.

2   **AT RISE:**   Enter Queen and Polonius

3

4   POLONIUS: He will come straight. Look you lay home to him:

5   Tell him his pranks have been too broad to bear with,

6   And that your Grace hath screen'd and stood between

7   Much heat and him. I'll sconce me [1] even here.

8   Pray you, be round [2] with him.

9   HAMLET: *(Within)* Mother, mother, mother!

10   QUEEN: I'll warrant you; fear me not: — withdraw,

11   I hear him coming. *(POLONIUS goes behind the arras. Enter*

12   *HAMLET)*

13   HAMLET: Now, mother, what's the matter?

14   QUEEN: Hamlet, thou hast thy father much offended.

15   HAMLET: Mother, you have my father much offended.

16   QUEEN: Come, come, you answer with an idle tongue.

17   HAMLET: Go, go, you question with a wicked tongue.

18   QUEEN: Why, how now, Hamlet!

19   HAMLET: What's the matter now?

20   QUEEN: Have you forgot me?

21   HAMLET: No, by the rood, [3] not so:

22   You are the queen, your husband's brother's wife;

23   And — would it were not so! — you are my mother.

24   QUEEN: Nay, then, I'll set those to you that can speak.

25   HAMLET: Come, come, and sit you down; you shall not

26   budge;

27   You go not till I set you up a glass

28   Where you may see the inmost part of you.

29   QUEEN: What wilt thou do? thou wilt not murder me? —

30   Help, help, ho!

31   POLONIUS: *(Behind)* What, ho! help, help, help!

32

33   [1] *sconce: hide.*

34   [2] *round: straightforward.*

35   [3] *rood: cross.*

1	**HAMLET:** *(Drawing)* **How now! a rat? Dead for a ducat, dead!**
2	*(Makes a pass through the arras.)*
3	**POLONIUS:** *(Behind)* **O, I am slain!** *(Falls and dies.)*
4	**QUEEN: O me, what hast thou done?**
5	**HAMLET: Nay, I know not: is it the king?**
6	**QUEEN: O, what a rash and bloody deed is this!**
7	**HAMLET: A bloody deed! — almost as bad, good mother,**
8	**As kill a king, and marry with his brother.**
9	**QUEEN: As kill a king!**
10	**HAMLET: Ay, lady 'twas my word. —** *(Lifts up the arras and*
11	*sees POLONIUS.)*
12	**Thou wretched, rash, intruding fool, farewell!**
13	**I took thee for thy better: take thy fortune;**
14	**Thou find'st to be too busy is some danger. —**
15	**Leave wringing of your hands: peace; sit you down,**
16	**And let me wring your heart: for so I shall,**
17	**If it be made of penetrable stuff;**
18	**If damned custom have not brazed it so,**
19	**That it is proof and bulwark against sense.**
20	**QUEEN: What have I done, that thou darest wag thy tongue**
21	**In noise so rude against me?**
22	**HAMLET: Such an act**
23	**That blurs the grace and blush of modesty;**
24	**Calls virtue hypocrite; takes off the rose**
25	**From the fair forehead of an innocent love,**
26	**And sets a blister there; makes marriage-vows**
27	**As false as dicers' oaths: O, such a deed**
28	**As from the body of contraction plucks**
29	**The very soul; and sweet religion makes**
30	**A rhapsody of words: heaven's face doth glow;**
31	**Yea, this solidity and compound mass,**
32	**With tristful[1] visage, as against the doom,**
33	**Is thought-sick at the act.**
34	
35	[1]*tristful: sad.*

1   QUEEN: Ay me, what act,
2   That roars so loud, and thunders in the index?
3   HAMLET: Look here, upon this picture and on this,
4   The counterfeit presentment of two brothers.
5   See, what a grace was seated on this brow;
6   Hyperion's curls; the front of Jove himself;
7   An eye like Mars, to threaten and command;
8   A station like the herald Mercury
9   New-lighted on a heaven-kissing hill;
10   A combination and a form indeed,
11   Where every god did seem to set his seal,
12   To give the world assurance of a man:
13   This was your husband. — Look you now, what follows:
14   Here is your husband; like a mildew'd ear,
15   Blasting his wholesome brother. Have you eyes?
16   Could you on this fair mountain leave to feed.
17   And batten on this moor? Ha! have you eyes?
18   You cannot call it love; for at your age
19   The hey-day in the blood is tame, it's humble,
20   And waits upon the judgment: and what judgment
21   Would step from this to this? Sense, sure, you have,
22   Else could you not have motion: but, sure, that sense
23   Is apoplext:[1] for madness would not err;
24   Nor sense to ecstasy was ne'er so thrall'd
25   But it reserved some quantity of choice,
26   To serve in such a difference. What devil was't
27   That thus hath cozen'd[2] you to hoodman-blind?
28   Eyes without feeling, feeling without sight,
29   Ears without hands or eyes, smelling sans all,
30   Or but a sickly part of one true sense
31   Could not so mope.
32   O shame! where is thy blush? Rebellious hell,
33
34   [1]*apoplext: paralyzed.*
35   [2]*cozen'd: tricked.*

```
1        If thou canst mutine in a matron's bones,
2        To flaming youth let virtue be as wax,
3        And melt in her own fire: proclaim no shame
4        When the compulsive ardour gives the charge,
5        Since frost itself as actively doth burn,
6        And reason pandars will.
7   QUEEN:  O Hamlet, speak no more:
8        Thou turn'st mine eyes into my very soul;
9        And there I see such black and grained spots
10       As will not leave their tinct.
11  HAMLET:  Nay, but to live
12       In the rank sweet of an enseamed bed,
13       Stew'd in corruption, honeying and making love
14       Over the nasty sty, —
15  QUEEN:  O, speak to me no more;
16       These words, like daggers, enter in mine ears;
17       No more, sweet Hamlet!
18  HAMLET:  A murderer and a villain;
19       A slave that is not twentieth part the tithe
20       Of your precedent lord; a vice of kings;
21       A cutpurse of the empire and the rule,
22       That from a shelf the previous diadem stole,
23       And put it in his pocket!
24  QUEEN:  No more!
25  HAMLET:  A king of shreds and patches, — *(Enter GHOST)*
26       Save me, and hover o'er me with your wings,
27       You  heavenly  guards! — What  would  your  gracious
28          figure?
29  QUEEN:  Alas, he's mad!
30  HAMLET:  Do you not come your tardy son to chide,
31       That, lapsed in time and passion, lets go by
32       Th'important acting of your dread command?
33       O, say!
34  GHOST:  Do not forget: this visitation
35       Is but to whet thy almost blunted purpose.
```

1	But, look, amazement on thy mother sits:
2	O, step between her and her fighting soul, —
3	Conceit in weakest bodies strongest works, —
4	Speak to her, Hamlet.
5	HAMLET: How is it with you, lady?
6	QUEEN: Alas, how is't with you,
7	That you do bend your eye on vacancy,
8	And with th'incorporal air do hold discourse?
9	Forth at your eyes your spirits wildly peep;
10	And, as the sleeping soldiers in th'alarm,
11	Your bedded hair, like life in excrements,
12	Start up, and stand an end. O gentle son,
13	Upon the heat and flame of thy distemper
14	Sprinkle cool patience. Whereon do you look?
15	HAMLET: On him, on him! Look you, how pale he glares!
16	His form and cause conjoin'd, preaching to stones,
17	Would make them capable. — Do not look upon me;
18	Lest with this piteous action you convert
19	My stern effects: then what I have to do
20	Will want true color; tears perchance for blood.
21	QUEEN: To whom do you speak this?
22	HAMLET: Do you see nothing there?
23	QUEEN: Nothing at all; yet all that is I see.
24	HAMLET: Nor did you nothing hear?
25	QUEEN: No, nothing but ourselves.
26	HAMLET: Why, look you there! look, how it steals away!
27	My father, in his habit as he lived!
28	Look, where he goes, even now, out at the portal! *(Exit*
29	*GHOST)*
30	QUEEN: This is the very coinage of your brain:
31	This bodiless creation ecstasy
32	Is very cunning in.
33	HAMLET: Ecstasy!
34	My pulse, as yours, doth temperately keep time,
35	And makes as healthful music: it is not madness

1	That I have utter'd: bring me to the test,
2	And I the matter will re-word; which madness
3	Would gambol from. Mother, for love of grace,
4	Lay not that flattering unction to your soul,
5	That not your trespass, but my madness speaks:
6	It will but skin and film the ulcerous place,
7	Whilst rank corruption, mining all within,
8	Infects unseen. Confess yourself to heaven;
9	Repent what's past; avoid what is to come;
10	And do not spread the compost on the weeds,
11	To make them ranker. Forgive me this my virtue;
12	For in the fatness of these pursy times
13	Virtue itself of vice must pardon beg,
14	Yea, curb and woo for leave to do him good.
15	QUEEN: O Hamlet, thou hast cleft my heart in twain.
16	HAMLET: O, throw away the worser part of it,
17	And live the purer with the other half.
18	Good night: but go not to my uncle's bed;
19	Assume a virtue, if you have it not.
20	That monster, custom, who all sense doth eat,
21	Of habits devil, is angel yet in this,
22	That to the use of actions fair and good
23	He likewise gives a frock or livery,
24	That aptly is put on. Refrain tonight;
25	And that shall lend a kind of easiness
26	To the next abstinence: the next more easy;
27	For use almost can change the stamp of nature,
28	And either master the devil, or throw him out
29	With wondrous potency. Once more, good night:
30	And when you are desirous to be blest,
31	I'll blessing beg of you. — For this same lord, *(Pointing to*
32	*POLONIUS)*
33	I do repent: but heaven hath pleased it so,
34	To punish me with this, and this with me,
35	That I must be their scourge and minister.

1	I will bestow him, and will answer well
2	The death I gave him. So, again, good night. —
3	I must be cruel, only to be kind:
4	Thus bad begins, and worse remains behind. —
5	One word more, good lady.
6	QUEEN: What shall I do?
7	HAMLET: Not this, by no means, that I bid you do:
8	Let the bloat king tempt you again to bed;
9	Pinch wanton on your cheek; call you his mouse;
10	And let him, for a pair of reechy kisses,
11	Or paddling in your neck with his damn'd fingers,
12	Make you to ravel all this matter out,
13	That I essentially am not in madness,
14	But mad in craft. 'Twere good you let him know;
15	For who, that's but a queen, fair, sober, wise,
16	Would from a paddock,[1] from a bat, a gib,[2]
17	Such dear concernings hide? who would do so?
18	No, in despite of sense and secrecy,
19	Unpeg the basket on the house's top,
20	Let the birds fly, and, like the famous ape,
21	To try conclusions, in the basket creep,
22	And break your own neck down.
23	QUEEN: Be thou assured, if words be made of breath
24	And breath of life, I have no life to breathe
25	What thou hast said to me.
26	HAMLET: I must to England; you know that?
27	QUEEN: Alack,
28	I had forgot: 'tis so concluded on.
29	HAMLET: There's letters seal'd: and my two school-
30	fellows, —
31	Whom I will trust as I will adders fang'd, —
32	They bear the mandate; they must sweep my way,
33	
34	[1]*paddock: frog.*
35	[2]*gib: cat.*

1   And marshal me to knavery. Let it work;
2   For 'tis the sport to have the enginer
3   Hoist with his own petar: and 't shall go hard
4   But I will delve one yard below their mines,
5   And blow them at the moon: O, 'tis most sweet
6   When in one line two crafts directly meet. —
7   This man shall set me packing:
8   I'll lug the guts into the neighbor room. —
9   Mother, good night. — Indeed, this counsellor
10   Is now most still, most secret, and most grave,
11   Who was in life a foolish prating knave.
12   Come, sir, to draw toward an end with you. —
13   Good night, mother. *(Exeunt severally, HAMLET tugging in*
14   *POLONIUS)*
15
16
17
18
19
20
21
22
23
24
25
26
27
28
29
30
31
32
33
34
35

Hamlet
Act IV, Scene 7

MAJOR CHARACTERS

King Claudius — Hamlet's uncle who murdered Hamlet's father and married his mother. He is becoming increasingly paranoid of Hamlet, and he suspects him of avenging his father's death by killing him.

Laertes — son of the late Polonius, who was killed by Hamlet

MINOR CHARACTER

Gertrude — mother of Hamlet and wife to Claudius

EXTRA — Messenger

The King has told Laertes that Hamlet killed his father and wants to kill him, Claudius. He further explains that he cannot apprehend Hamlet for the crime for two reasons: Queen Gertrude, to whom he is married, is completely devoted to her son; secondly, he could not expect to receive full public support because the townspeople love Hamlet and he must conceal the fact that he murdered Hamlet's father.

A messenger delivers letters from Hamlet: one for the King and one for the Queen. In his letter, the King learns that Hamlet is returning to Denmark; he immediately engages Laertes in a plot to kill Hamlet. He says that he will arrange a fencing match between the two and that Laertes will use a foil with an unblunted point. To assure victory, Laertes states that he will dip the point of his rapier in deadly poison. Claudius adds a second means of insuring Hamlet's death: he will have prepared, and available, a cup of poisoned wine for Hamlet to drink in the event that Laertes does not stab him in the duel.

Gertrude enters and informs Laertes that his sister Ophelia has drowned. (She was weaving garlands and hanging them on the limbs of a willow tree when a limb broke and she fell in the stream.) Laertes tries to control his grief but cannot do so.

1   *SETTING:*   Another room in the castle.

2   *AT RISE:*   Enter King and Laertes.

3

4   KING: Now must your conscience my acquittance seal,

5   And you must put me in your heart for friend,

6   Sith[1] you have heard, and with a knowing ear,

7   That he which hath your noble father slain

8   Pursued my life.

9   LAERTES: It well appears: — but tell me

10   Why you proceeded not against these feats,

11   So crimeful and so capital in nature,

12   As by your safety, wisdom, all things else,

13   You mainly were stirr'd up.[2]

14   KING: O, for two special reasons;

15   Which may to you, perhaps, seem much unsinew'd.

16   But yet to me th' are strong. The queen his mother

17   Lives almost by his looks; and for myself, —

18   My virtue or my plague, be it either which, —

19   She's so conjunctive to my life and soul,

20   That, as the star moves not but in his sphere,

21   I could not but by her. The other motive,

22   Why to a public count I might not go,

23   Is the great love the general gender bear him;

24   Who, dipping all his faults in their affection,

25   Would, like the spring that turneth wood to stone,

26   Convert his gyves to graces; so that my arrows,

27   Too slightly timber'd for so loud a wind,

28   Would have reverted to my bow again,

29   And not where I had aim'd them.

30   LAERTES: And so have I a noble father lost;

31   A sister driven into desperate terms, —

32   Whose worth, if praises may go back again,

33

34   [1]*Sith: since.*

35   [2]*stirr'd up: involved.*

1   Stood challenger on mount of all the age

2   For her perfections: — but my revenge will come.

3 KING: Break not your sleeps for that: you must not think

4   That we are made of stuff so flat and dull,

5   That we can let our beard be shook with danger,

6   And think it pastime. You shortly shall hear more:

7   I loved your father, and we love ourself;

8   And that, I hope, will teach you to imagine — *(Enter a*

9   *MESSENGER)*

10   How now! what news?

11 MESSENGER: Letters my lord, from Hamlet:

12   This to your majesty; this to the queen.

13 KING: From Hamlet! who brought them?

14 MESSENGER: Sailors, my lord, they say; I saw them not:

15   They were given me by Claudio, — he received them

16   Of him that brought them.

17 KING: Laertes, you shall hear them. —

18   Leave us. *(Exit MESSENGER. KING reads.)* High and

19   mighty, — You shall know I am set naked on your

20   kingdom. Tomorrow shall I beg leave to see your kingly

21   eyes: when I shall, first asking your pardon thereunto,

22   recount the occasion of my sudden and more strange

23   return. Hamlet.

24   What should this mean? Are all the rest come back?

25   Or is it some abuse,[1] and no such thing?

26 LAERTES: Know you the hand?

27 KING: 'Tis Hamlet's character: — "Naked," —

28   And in a postscript here, he says, "alone."

29   Can you advise me?

30 LAERTES: I'm lost in it, my lord. But let him come;

31   It warms the very sickness in my heart,

32   That I shall live and tell him to his teeth,

33   "Thus diddest thou."

34

35   [1] *abuse: deception.*

1   KING: If it be so, Laertes, —
2   As how should it be so? how otherwise? —
3   Will you be ruled by me?
4   LAERTES: Ay, my lord;
5   So you will not o'errule me to a peace.
6   KING: To thine own peace. If he be now return'd, —
7   As checking at his voyage, and that he means
8   No more to undertake it, — I will work him
9   To an exploit, now ripe in my device,
10   Under the which he shall not choose but fall:
11   And for his death no wind of blame shall breathe;
12   But even his mother shall uncharge the practice,
13   And call it accident.
14   LAERTES: My lord, I will be ruled;
15   The rather, if you could devise it so,
16   That I might be the organ.
17   KING: It falls right.
18   You have been talkt of since your travel much,
19   And that in Hamlet's hearing, for a quality
20   Wherein, they say, you shine: your sum of parts
21   Did not together pluck such envy from him,
22   As did that one; and that, in my regard,
23   Of the unworthiest siege.
24   LAERTES: What part is that, my lord?
25   KING: A very riband in the cap of youth,
26   Yet needful too; for youth no less becomes
27   The light and careless livery that it wears
28   Than settled age his sables and his weeds,
29   Importing health and graveness. — Two months since,
30   Here was a gentleman of Normandy, —
31   I've seen myself, and served against, the French,
32   And they can well on horseback: but this gallant
33   Had witchcraft in't; he grew unto his seat;
34   And to such wondrous doing brought his horse,
35   As he had been incorpsed and demi-natured

1   With the brave beast: so far he topt my thought,

2   That I, in forgery of shapes and tricks,

3   Come short of what he did.

4 LAERTES: A Norman was't?

5 KING: A Norman.

6 LAERTES: Upon my life, Lamond.

7 KING: The very same.

8 LAERTES: I know him well: he is the brooch, indeed,

9   And gem of all the nation.

10 KING: He made confession of you;

11   And gave you such a masterly report,

12   For art and exercise in your defence,

13   And for your rapier most especially,

14   That he cried out, 'twould be a sight indeed,

15   If one could match you: the scrimers of their nation,

16   He swore, had neither motion, guard, nor eye,

17   If you opposed them. Sir, this report of his

18   Did Hamlet so envenom with his envy,

19   That he could nothing do but wish and beg

20   Your sudden coming o'er, to play with him.

21   Now, out of this, —

22 LAERTES: What out of this, my lord?

23 KING: Laertes, was your father dear to you?

24   Or are you like the painting of a sorrow,

25   A face without a heart?

26 LAERTES: Why ask you this?

27 KING: Not that I think you did not love your father;

28   But that I know love is begun by time;

29   And that I see, in passages of proof,

30   Time qualifies the spark and fire of it.

31   There lives within the very flame of love

32   A kind of wick or snuff that will abate it;

33   And nothing is at a like goodness still;

34   For goodness, growing to a plurisy,

35   Dies in his own too-much: that we would do,

1	We should do when we would; for this "would" changes,
2	And hath abatements and delays as many
3	As there are tongues, are hands, are accidents;
4	And then this "should" is like a spendthrift sigh,
5	That hurts by easing. But, to th'quick o'th' ulcer: —
6	Hamlet comes back: what would you undertake,
7	To show yourself your father's son in deed
8	More than in words?
9	LAERTES: To cut his throat i'th'church.
10	KING: No place, indeed, should murder sanctuarize;
11	Revenge should have no bounds. But, good Laertes,
12	Will you do this, keep close within your chamber.
13	Hamlet return'd shall know you are come home:
14	We'll put on those shall praise your excellence,
15	And set a double varnish on the fame
16	The Frenchman gave you; bring you, in fine, together,
17	And wager on your heads: he, being remiss,
18	Most generous, and free from all contriving,
19	Will not peruse the foils; so that, with ease,
20	Or with a little shuffling, you may choose
21	A sword unbated, and, in a pass of practice,
22	Requite him for your father.
23	LAERTES: I will do't:
24	And for that purpose I'll anoint my sword.
25	I bought an unction of a mountebank,
26	So mortal, that but dip a knife in it.
27	Where it draws blood no cataplasm so rare,
28	Collected from all simples that have virtue
29	Under the moon, can save the thing from death
30	That is but scratcht withal: I'll touch my point
31	With this contagion, that, if I gall him slightly,
32	It may be death.
33	KING: Let's further think of this;
34	Weigh what convenience both of time and means
35	May fit us to our shape; if this should fail,

1   And that our drift look through our bad performance,
2   'Twere better not assay'd: therefore this project
3   Should have a back or second, that might hold,
4   If this should blast in proof. Soft! — let me see: —
5   We'll make a solemn wager on your cunnings, —
6   I ha't:
7   When in your motion you are hot and dry, —
8   As make your bouts more violent to that end, —
9   And that he calls for drink, I'll have prepared him
10   A chalice for the nonce; whereon but sipping,
11   If he by chance escape your venom'd stuck,
12   Our purpose may hold there. But stay! what noise? —
13   *(Enter QUEEN)*
14   How now, sweet queen!
15 QUEEN: One woe doth tread upon another's heel,
16   So fast they follow: — your sister's drown'd, Laertes.
17 LAERTES: Drown'd! O, where?
18 QUEEN: There is a willow grows aslant a brook,
19   That shows his hoar leaves in a glassy stream;
20   There with fantastic garlands did she come
21   Of crow-flowers, nettles, daisies, and long purples
22   That liberal shepherds give a grosser name,
23   But our cold maids do dead men's fingers call them:
24   There, on the pendent boughs her coronet weeds
25   Clambering to hang, an envious sliver broke;
26   When down her weedy trophies and herself
27   Fell in the weeping brook. Her clothes spread wide,
28   And, mermaid-like, awhile they bore her up;
29   Which time she chanted snatches of old tunes,
30   As one incapable of her own distress,
31   Or like a creature native and indued
32   Unto that element: but long it could not be
33   Till that her garments, heavy with their drink,
34   Pull'd the poor wretch from her melodious lay
35   To muddy death.

1   LAERTES: Alas, then, she is drown'd?

2   QUEEN: Drown'd, drown'd.

3   LAERTES: Too much of water hast thou, poor Ophelia,

4   And therefore I forbid my tears: but yet

5   It is our trick, nature her custom holds,

6   Let shame say what it will: when these are gone,

7   The woman will be out. — Adieu, my lord:

8   I have a speech of fire, that fain would blaze,

9   But that this folly douts it. *(Exit LAERTES)*

10   KING: Let's follow, Gertrude:

11   How much I had to do to calm his rage!

12   Now fear I this will give it start again;

13   Therefore let's follow. *(They exit.)*

14

15

16

17

18

19

20

21

22

23

24

25

26

27

28

29

30

31

32

33

34

35

ABOUT THE AUTHOR

Michael Wilson graduated from California State University, Chico, in 1974 with a degree in English; he received his teaching credential from the same institution the following year and has done graduate work at California State University, Fresno, and at Fresno Pacific College. He has been teaching in the Visalia Unified School District for 18 years and has been teaching drama at Golden West High School for 12 years. He currently teaches three levels of drama and also American Literature and Advanced Composition/Grammar. He directs and produces the plays for Golden West High School and has produced over 30 shows (including musicals) thus far.

Along with his teaching, he is a musician who performs in a local rock band, Thin Ice, and has worked as a part-time musician for over 20 years, performing in different parts of California, Las Vegas, and at Super Bowl XXIII.

ORDER FORM

MERIWETHER PUBLISHING LTD.
P.O. BOX 7710
COLORADO SPRINGS, CO 80933
TELEPHONE: (719) 594-4422

Please send me the following books:

_____**Scenes From Shakespeare #TT-B120**   **$9.95**
edited by **Michael Wilson**
Fifteen cuttings for the classroom

_____**Scenes and Monologs From the Best**
New Plays #TT-B140   **$14.95**
edited by **Roger Ellis**
An anthology of new American plays

_____**The Scenebook for Actors #TT-B177**   **$14.95**
by **Norman A. Bert**
Great monologs and dialogs for auditions

_____**Scenes That Happen #TT-B156**   **$9.95**
by **Mary Krell-Oishi**
Dramatized snapshots of high school life

_____**Theatre Alive #TT-B178**   **$24.95**
by **Norman A. Bert**
An introductory anthology of world drama

_____**Winning Monologs for Young Actors #TT-B127** **$9.95**
by **Peg Kehret**
Honest-to-life monologs for actors

_____**Theatre Games for Young Performers #TT-B188** **$9.95**
by **Maria C. Novelly**
Improvisations and exercises for developing acting skills

I understand that I may return any book
for a full refund if not satisfied.

NAME: _____

ORGANIZATION NAME: _____

ADDRESS: _____

CITY: _____ STATE: _____ ZIP: _____

PHONE: _____

☐ **Check Enclosed**
☐ **Visa or Mastercard #**_____

Signature: _____   *Expiration*
Date: _____
(required for Visa/Mastercard orders)

COLORADO RESIDENTS: Please add 3% sales tax.
SHIPPING: Include $1.50 for the first book and 50¢ for each additional book ordered.

☐ *Please send me a copy of your complete catalog of books and plays.*